HEROES OF
STOCK CAR RACING

Exciting profiles of some of racing's greatest drivers, illustrated with action photographs. Included are Lee and Richard Petty, Fireball Roberts, Junior Johnson, A.J. Foyt, LeeRoy Yarbrough, Cale Yarborough, Bobby Allison, David Pearson, and others.

illustrated with photographs

HEROES OF
STOCK CAR RACING

by Bill Libby

RANDOM HOUSE
NEW YORK

PHOTOGRAPH CREDITS: Darlington Raceway, 4–5, 21, 43, 52, 56, 60, 95; Daytona International Speedway, endpapers, 8, 14–15; Dodge News Photo, 16; Ford Motor Company, 71; Bill Libby, 19, 26, 44, 70, 110, 133; Michigan International Speedway, 31; NASCAR, back of front endpapers, 82–83, 101, 115; Official Ontario Motor Speedway Photo, 91; Bob Tronolone, 2–3, 62–63, 100, 130, 136–137; United Press International, 34, 39, 47, 75, 107, 118, 126; Wide World Photos, 51, 67, 84, 87, 90, 103, 123, 145, 147.

COVER: Photo by Al Satterwhite (Camera 5)

Library of Congress Cataloging in Publication Data
Libby, Bill.   Heroes of stock car racing.   (Random House sports library; no. 5)
SUMMARY: Brief biographies of twelve stock car drivers including Lee and Richard Petty, Pops Turner, A. J. Foyt, and Bobby Allison.
1. Automobile racing—Biography—Juvenile literature.   [1. Automobile racing—Biography] I. Title.
GV1032.A1L52   796.7'2'0922 [B]   [920]   74-24763
ISBN 0-394-82994-8   ISBN 0-394-92994-2 lib. hdg.

Manufactured in the United States of America   1 2 3 4 5 6 7 8 9 0

For **Arthur Freudenberg,**

a good ol' boy himself, who loves sports.

The author wishes to thank all the drivers for all the interviews he has received over the years. He wishes also to thank Philip Holmer and others at NASCAR; Dick Jordan and others at USAC; Dusty Brandel and others of the AARWBA; Parnelli Jones, Jim Cook, Bob Thomas, Jack Matthews, Sue Ovitt and others at Ontario Motor Speedway; the staff at Daytona International Raceway, and the staffs at all the other major racing tracks across the country. Finally, the author wishes also to thank all the writers whose work contributed to his knowledge of this sport and all the photographers whose work appears with this book.

CONTENTS

INTRODUCTION

Lee and Richard Petty are father and son in the most famous and successful family in stock car racing. Yet in the backyard of the sprawling layout where the Pettys live and work, there is a junkpile of wrecked racing cars.

Only a few steps from the shop where the Pettys put together tomorrow's winning cars, they can see the remains of yesterday's failures. The scrap-heap is there to remind the family how hard it was to get to the top of their sport and how hard it is to stay there.

According to legend, stock car racing began in the South with men whose business was to distill and sell whiskey illegally—without getting a federal license and without paying liquor taxes.

The outlaw distillers—called bootleggers—needed "runners," men who could carry the whiskey from the backwoods stills to customers in town. It was a hazardous job, since local sheriffs, state police and feared federal revenue agents all were on the watch for illegal shipments. The runners learned to soup up their cars and keep them in tune. And they became expert drivers, able to run at top speed without lights in the dead of night on back-country roads. When they did meet a lawman, these skilled outlaws usually could evade or outrun their pursuer.

When they weren't running whiskey to market, the owners of these souped-up cars amused themselves by racing each other, first on out-of-the-way roads and later on crude dirt tracks. As whiskey-running became more dangerous and less profitable, the owners of the small oval tracks began to organize the races and charge curious spectators an admission fee. The cars were called stock cars or "stockers," because on the outside they looked like everyday passenger cars which any dealer would have in stock—Fords, Chevys, Dodges, Pontiacs and the like.

Gradually, a new motor sport was born. In the late 1940s organizations were springing up throughout the South to build tracks, sponsor races and set fair standards of competition. The most successful of these organizations was the National Association for Stock Car Auto Racing, soon known as NASCAR. Its founder, Bill France, was a former driver, mechanic, car owner and promoter in Daytona Beach, Florida, where various kinds of cars had been racing—on a sandy, open beach—since the turn of the century. France served as president of NASCAR until 1962 and was succeeded by his son, Bill, Jr.

The first race on the new NASCAR Grand National circuit was run in June 1949 in Charlotte, North Carolina. Soon the organization was sponsoring races for many kinds of cars, but the Grand National series, for the big stock cars with the biggest engines, brought out the best mechanics and drivers and attracted the largest crowds. By the 1970s, all types of auto racing drew more paying spectators in the United States than any other sport except horse racing, and the largest share of these huge crowds followed the stockers.

Today there are 45 to 50 Grand National events a year, run on all kinds of tracks from the half-mile dirt ovals to the 2½-mile paved super-speedway at Daytona Beach. A majority of NASCAR races still are run in the South, but an increasing number are run in other parts of the country from New York to California. Twelve tracks qualify as super-speedways. All are a mile or more long and are paved. Nearly all are banked high, especially in the corners, allowing stock car drivers to achieve speeds up to 200 miles per hour.

The oldest of the big tracks is Darlington, which was opened in the tobacco country of South Carolina in 1950. Then in 1959 Bill France of NASCAR built Daytona International Speedway in Florida. Other big tracks followed in rapid succession. Most of these tracks run two big races a year, one in the late winter or spring and the other in the summer or fall. The current list of super-speedways and races can be found on the following page.

Contests on the big tracks are all between 400 and 600 miles long. However, many main events on lesser tracks are between 100 and 250 miles. Such races may be as grueling as the longer races because 250 miles on a half-mile track means 500 tight laps, where the driver must wrestle his steering wheel to the left almost continuously.

Much of the appeal of stock cars is that they look like

Super-Speedways*

TRACK	FIRST RACE	SECOND RACE
Alabama International Speedway Talladega, Alabama 2.6 miles, oval	May Talladega 500	August Winston 500
Atlanta International Speedway Hampton, Georgia 1.52 miles, oval	March Atlanta 500	July Dixie 500
Charlotte Motor Speedway Charlotte, North Carolina 1.5 miles, oval	May World 600	October National 500
Darlington International Raceway Darlington, South Carolina 1.36 miles, oval	April Rebel 500	September Southern 500
Daytona International Speedway Daytona Beach, Florida 2.5 miles, oval	February Daytona 500	July Firecracker 400
Dover Downs International Speedway Dover, Delaware 1 mile, oval	May Mason-Dixon 500	September Delaware 500
Michigan International Speedway Irish Hills, Michigan 2.04 miles, oval	June Motor State 400	August Yankee 400
North Carolina Motor Speedway Rockingham, North Carolina 1.01 miles, oval	March Carolina 500	October American 500
Ontario Motor Speedway Ontario, California 2.5 miles, oval	March Miller 500	November Times 500
Pocono International Raceway Long Pond, Pennsylvania 2.5 miles, oval		August Pocono 500
Riverside International Raceway Riverside, California 2.62 miles, irregular road course	June Tuborg 400	
Texas World Speedway College Station, Texas 2 miles, oval	June Alamo 500	October Texas 500

* Paved tracks of one mile or more used annually for a NASCAR event of 400 miles or more. The names, distances and dates of some races have changed over the years.

the family car people drive on the highways. But in fact, they really are not much more than the shell of a family car. The frames have been beefed up for safety and the engines souped up for speed. The most imaginative and skilled mechanics in the business build stock car engines to get maximum power and reliability, limited only by the standards set by NASCAR or other sanctioning bodies.

NASCAR also sets the racing rules. When an accident clogs the track, yellow caution signals alert the drivers to slow down, and the rules forbid passing. On rare occasions a race may have to be stopped because of bad weather or a major accident.

Running speeds on the NASCAR circuit are higher than at Indianapolis or in any other form of closed-course racing. Because of these high speeds, the cars cannot always be controlled, and their engines sometimes explode, spewing broken pieces all over the track. Like other motor sports, stock car racing is dangerous. But because stock cars have reinforced frames and provide complete enclosure for the driver, they often bang into each other and even crash into barriers without causing serious injuries. They are far safer than the smaller open racers that run at Indianapolis and on the international Grand Prix trail.

And the stockers achieve their amazing safety record even though they offer the closest competition of any races in the world. It is not unusual for cars to be bumper-to-bumper for 500 miles or side-by-side as they roar into the home stretch.

The men who drive stockers, keeping control of them at top speeds of 200 miles per hour in traffic conditions that resemble the freeway at rush hour, are amazing

athletes. They must have not only the strength, coordination, reflexes and intelligence of performers in other sports, but also the cool courage to perform in constant danger.

Of those who start out to become stock car heroes, many never succeed. It takes talent, years of experience, top equipment and lots of luck to reach the list of top money winners. In 1972 a driver named Neil "Soapy" Castles won a 100-mile race on a half-mile track in Greenville, South Carolina. It was his first victory after

19 years of competition and 458 races on the Grand National tour. There are dozens like him.

But this is a book about the superstars of this spectacular sport, the men who have had the talent, determination and equipment to win race after race. It takes a lot to survive in a sport where dozens of younger drivers are always challenging at 180 miles per hour. As the Pettys recall when they look at their scrap-pile, racing brings frustration even to the most successful in this fiercest of sports.

Above, Lee Petty lets his son Richard sit behind the wheel in 1953. Fourteen years later, below, Dad gets a chance to try his son's car.

LEE and RICHARD PETTY

Like Father, Like Son

The first time Richard Petty ever got into a stock car race, he did not drive, he rode—on the hood of his father's car. Richard was 13 and his father, Lee Petty, was driving a race on a muddy track at High Point, North Carolina. Lee's windshield had coated over with mud so he could not see except by sticking his head out the side window. When he pulled into the pits, Richard grabbed a rag and started to clean the windshield, then hopped on the hood so that he could reach all the way across.

Lee was watching another crew member fill up the gas tank, and when that operation was finished, he slammed his car into gear and roared away. He was halfway around the tiny track before he spotted his son on the hood, hanging on desperately. The next time around, he pulled back into the pits, lingering only long enough for

Richard to hop off, then tore out again. He went on to win.

Years later, Richard recalled the incident and said, "It's better inside, with seat belts on."

Richard's first "race" happened in 1950, only a few years after his father Lee first took up competitive driving. During the next 25 years, the Pettys would become stock car racing's first family, dominating the sport for two generations and setting records that may never be broken.

The Pettys live in Level Cross, North Carolina, a town too small to have a post office. Their mailing address is in Randleman, but Randleman is so small that its telephone exchange is in High Point, which is not the largest place in the state, either. To get to Level Cross a visitor must take the main highway, turn off onto a small road, then onto a smaller road. When he gets to a general store with a Coca Cola sign and a gas station out front, he finds still another road, a dusty, bumpy little cow path, and takes that to the Petty spread.

Lee Petty and his wife live in one house; their sons Richard and Maurice and their nephew Dale Inman live with their families in other houses all arranged in a semi-circle facing the center of activity, the garage where the Petty cars are prepared for racing. Lee oversees the team, Richard does the driving, Dale is the team manager, and Maurice is the engine specialist. It is isolated, peaceful and quiet, except when they fire up one of those racing engines. During the racing season, one or two of the cars is hauled away almost every week, on the way to a race. Racing is the Pettys' business.

In 1947 stock car racing was just beginning to boom. Lee Petty was a tough, flinty sort who had been helping

The Petty family in 1960: Richard, Lee and Maurice with their wives.

build and repair cars other men were racing. He was 33 years old, hardly an age when most men take up racing. But Lee had an itch to try driving. "We had a garage," he recalled. "We built a lot of hot rods and specialized in tune-ups. I used to bang up cars on the back roads, but I'd never driven in a race. One day they had a race at Greensboro, North Carolina. I had it in my mind that someday I'd try a race, and that day I said I thought I'd give her a go. My brother said, 'You wanna try?' and I said, 'Why not?' So I did."

Lee flipped his car in his first start. When he drove in his first Daytona Beach race in 1949 he crashed. But he was a daring and determined man who did not discourage easily. He was brave, but also smart, and soon he was winning or finishing high in almost every race, piling up the points to place near the top in the drivers' standings each season.

For twelve straight seasons he never finished below fourth in the annual standings. He was first three times, second twice, third four times and fourth three times. He set the standard for victories, championships and consistency which were not surpassed until his son Richard bettered them. He raced in conditions far more difficult than today's and won in crude and cutthroat competition.

In 1954 Lee won the 250-miler on the beach at Daytona, a wild race in which the lead changed hands 35 times with the cars broadsliding across the sand surface at a torrid pace. That year, at the age of 40, he won his first driving title. He won again in 1958 (at 44) and again in 1959. That year he entered the first Daytona 500 on the new 2½-mile high-banked track enclosed by a sprawling stadium holding more than 100,000 spectators. The new track was a giant step forward for the stock car crowd, and the first Daytona 500 was a thriller.

Cotton Owens was the fastest qualifier with a speed above 143 miles per hour in his Pontiac, but he never led the race. Seven other drivers exchanged the lead 34 times through the long afternoon. Petty in an Oldsmobile and Johnny Beauchamp in a Thunderbird traded the lead eleven times the final 50 laps alone.

With the big crowd roaring, the two cars crossed the finish line side by side. There were no electronic photo-finish cameras then, and no one was sure who had won. The argument raged for three days while officials studied still photos and movies of the finish taken by fans. Finally they settled on one picture which showed Lee's car inches in front at the end.

At Charlotte that year, veteran driver Junior Johnson took up the whole track, preventing Petty's faster car

from passing. So Lee began to bang into the back of
Johnson's car. Petty's bumper bent Johnson's rear fender
in far enough to cut a tire and cause it to blow out. Junior
spun out, but missed the wall. He drove into the pits,
changed tires, got back on the track and rammed Petty
into the infield. The drivers scrambled out of their cars
and started to fight with their fists before the Charlotte
police chief broke it up.

Lee Petty was tough, but tough tactics on the track
eventually ended his career at Daytona in 1961. Once
again he was battling Beauchamp for the lead when they
collided, went out of control and sailed together over a
high guard rail. They spun through the air and landed in
a tangle of twisted metal, Beauchamp's car resting atop
Petty's mangled machine.

Maurice works on Lee's car before a race at Darlington in the 1950s.

Beauchamp escaped with minor injuries, but Petty was horribly hurt. His left kneecap was torn off and ribs were broken. He was carefully pried from the wreckage, placed on a stretcher, put in an ambulance and rushed to a hospital.

Doctors did not believe he would live long. His wife Elizabeth sat outside, pale with fear, praying for Lee's life. When Richard, who had already begun racing, went into the room, his father whispered, "Son, you take Momma on home and get the race car fixed up. I'll be all right. I'll come on home in a couple of days."

His son smiled. That was the way his father was. Forty days later Lee Petty came home. He had recovered, but his age was so advanced and his injuries so severe he would not drive regularly again.

Elizabeth Petty said, "When Lee had his accident, I wasn't surprised. I knew it could happen. That was a hard time, but it could've been worse. And when Richard was starting and Lee was so hard on him and people expected so much of him, I was upset, but we got through that time, too. I've been afraid for them, certainly. It's hard on any woman in any racing family. There's nothing we can do except wait and hope for the best. But it's no good trying to make a man not do what he wants to do. Maybe it started out wild with a bunch of bootleggers and all, but it's a real clean sport now. There's a lot of manliness to it, and my family has been somethin' special in it and have been able to stay real close because of it. I feel real proud."

Richard Lee Petty was born July 2, 1937. In high school he was an all-star football lineman and a good all-round athlete. He met his wife, Lynda, in high school, and married her soon after graduation. He attended business school for a while, but the family business was racing. His father had begun racing when Richard was ten, and had already won his first driving championship.

Still, Richard wasn't set on being a driver. He helped work on his dad's cars for a few years, and then one night when there were races at two different tracks and Lee could run only one, Richard asked to drive the other. Lee looked at him, thought about it a moment and then said, "Well, we have a few old cars laying around, so we'll fix one up and let you give her a try." So they did.

"I went to one and he went to the other," Richard remembered. "He didn't even see me run my first race. Anyway, I didn't win. I didn't win much for a while. But I had become a race driver. My daddy was a race driver, so I became a race driver. I grew up around cars. I been working on 'em since I was twelve years old and driving 'em since I was twenty-one and it's all I really know."

It's not easy to break into the big time on any racing circuit. Most young drivers must take any cars they can get and work their way up through small races on bad tracks for very little prize money. They try to make enough of a good impression to be offered a ride with one of the big teams whose cars are good enough to win consistently. A beginner may have to sleep in his car and eat sandwiches for every meal to save enough money for entry fees. And then his car may not go fast enough or last long enough to win. Many aspiring drivers—even those with the talent to become champions—have quit and gone home in disappointment.

Richard Petty had it easier. "The first couple of years I must have torn up about twenty or thirty thousand dollars of Dad's racing equipment," he remembered, "and I didn't bring home any prize money. But he just let

me find my way. Because of my dad's record, people
expected more of me than I could give them for a while.
If it'd been anybody else, I guess I'd've been shot out of
the saddle and never made it, but Dad carried me."

Richard drove his first race in 1958, and during his first
four years he sometimes drove against his father. Lee
never gave Richard a break on the track. In one race at
Atlanta, Richard took the checkered flag just ahead of
his dad and coasted right into the pits. Lee kept charging
around for another lap, then went to the officials and
demanded a recount, claiming that he was the winner
because the checkered flag had come out one lap too
early. They checked and Lee was right, so they took the
victory trophy away from Richard and gave it to his
father.

Lee snorted, "I don't reckon I regret it. When he wins,
he can have it, but he ain't gonna have it given to him."

After two years of learning, Richard won his first
Grand National race in 1960. Before the year was over,
he won two more and finished in the first five in almost
half of his 40 races. He finished second in the driving
standings.

"That was my third year on tour and I earned about
$35,000, which came close to getting Dad even on me,"
he said. "When Dad was seriously injured and had to
retire the following year, I knew I had to make the living
for the family, and it gave me a lot of desire."

Richard won only two races that year, but in 1962 and
'63 he won eight and 14, placing second in the drivers'
standings both years. He was on his way to the top. He
hadn't won any big super-speedway races, but he was
driving 40 or 50 events a year and placing high consistently.

Richard went all the way in 1964, his seventh season on the circuit. At season's start, he dominated the last 350 miles of the Daytona 500 to win easily at a new record speed of more than 154 miles per hour. That was his first super-speedway triumph, exactly ten years after his dad had won that first Daytona 500. Winning eight other races and placing among the top five finishers in 37 of 61 races, Richard won his first driving title and almost $100,000 in prize money.

Richard had been driving Plymouths for the Chrysler Corporation, but in 1965 NASCAR outlawed the big engine Plymouth was using, and the company withdrew from racing. Out of loyalty, Richard withdrew, too, and stayed away from NASCAR races through most of 1965. "I'm wastin' time," he said sadly. He tried his hand at drag racing instead, drawing big crowds and making big money, but far from the big time.

In April 1965 at a small drag strip in Georgia, he lost a wheel during a race and his car swerved into a ditch, up an embankment, over a fence and right into a knot of spectators, crashing into a small boy. As Richard sat dazed on the ground outside his smashed car, he pushed away people trying to help him, saying, "Just go see how that boy is." The boy was dead and others were hurt.

Years later, reflecting on the dangers of his business, Richard said, "Accidents are part of racing. They make it as safe as they can, but it can only be so safe. We all know we run the same risks. I know the next guy isn't going to quit if I get it, so I'm not goin' to quit if he gets it. If you're not of the sort of nature to live with it, you can't keep racing.

"The only thing I regret in racing is killing that little boy. It wasn't exactly my fault. It was one of those things that can happen in racing. And it was on a circuit that isn't as safe as ours. But I sure regret it."

Late in 1965, Petty and Chrysler returned to the Grand National circuit. Then in 1966 Richard started with a bang in the Daytona 500 at the start of the new season. Nearly 90,000 fans were on hand. They came from all over the country, pouring into the great arena to eat fried chicken, drink beer and soda pop, and watch the great drivers race.

There was no sun in sunny Florida on this day. Storm clouds blew over the stadium, but the cars were set to go anyway. At 12:30 P.M. the crowd came to its feet, and the drivers climbed into their cars, strapped themselves in,

Richard Petty chews on a damp rag during a pit stop.

and started their engines. After a lap or two behind the pace car in their starting positions, the green flag came down and the metal monsters roared away.

Petty pressed his Plymouth to the front and held it there for a few laps as the others strung out behind him. But his car was handling badly, causing unusual wear on the tires. He lost the lead, and after only 40 miles, far sooner than planned, Petty had to drive into the pits for new tires. For the next 200 miles, the lead passed back and forth. Paul Goldsmith led for 40 miles and Cale Yarborough for 70, but the pace was so fast that no driver could stay on top for long.

Meanwhile, Petty was struggling. He had to make more pit stops than anyone else to change tires, and at one point he had fallen two laps back, apparently hopelessly beaten. But he gradually learned how to handle the car and soon he was wrestling it around the oval faster than his foes, passing them and unlapping himself. His dad and the rest of his pit crew were ready with tires now, ready to get him in and out of the pits in a hurry.

Other cars were breaking down under the brutal pace. The car of Indianapolis champion A.J. Foyt came apart under him. Jim Hurtubise was throwing chunks of rubber off his tires large enough to shatter the windshields of two other cars. The drivers were wearing down, too. Slick Seltzer spun out. Bobby Isaac spun out. Hurtubise brushed Earl Balmer's car.

Petty pressed on daringly. The fans started to stand and wave white handkerchiefs at him as he passed, encouraging him on his mad dash. Just past the 280-mile mark, he pulled his car abreast of Yarborough's, passed, and drove into the lead as the crowd roared.

The skies were growing darker now, the threat of rain increasing. The lead became more valuable with every lap, because the race might be stopped at any time. Petty lengthened his lead. He pulled a quarter-mile in front of Yarborough, a half-mile, a mile, two miles. Then he had to go into the pits again, giving up a mile. He returned to the track and started to pull away again. Yarborough had to pit, too, but not needing tires, he was in and out fast.

The fans shivered as a moist breeze blew across the course. Fifty miles to go. Forty . . . thirty . . . twenty. It began to rain. The track got wet, and the big cars began to slide dangerously on the slick pavement. The officials huddled. Ten miles to go. The rain was pounding down now. The checkered flag was waved at Petty's car as he crossed the finish line, two laps short of the planned distance.

Richard Petty had made seven pit stops, changed eight tires, and come from two laps down to win by one lap in the fastest stock car race ever run. He had averaged more than 160 miles per hour for more than three hours to become the first man ever to win the Daytona 500 a second time.

"I never thought I had a chance until those fans started waving those white hankies at me. I figured if they thought I could make it, maybe I could," he said later.

He was on his way. He also won the Rebel 400 on the super-speedway at Darlington and the Dixie 400 at Atlanta.

In 1967, he won the Rebel 400 again. For the first time he took the Carolina 500 at Rockingham and the granddaddy of Grand National races, the Southern 500 at Darlington. As brilliant as he was on the big tracks, Richard shone even brighter on the small ovals. He won the Nashville 400 (400 1-mile laps) despite seven pit stops to change a dozen tires and a complete spin late in the race when one of his tires blew out. During one stretch he won ten Grand National races in a row.

When he won his 19th race of the season in the Sandpiper 200 at Columbia, South Carolina, he bettered the old record of 18 victories in a single season set by Tim Flock in 1952. He went on to win 27 races in 1967, which remains a record. He finished in the top five in eleven other races and easily won his second driving title, and a record $130,000 in prize money. Along the way, he won the 55th Grand National race of his career, breaking his father's record of 54.

In 1968, Richard won 16 more races, and earned nearly $90,000. In 1969, proving his skill on a road course, he won the Riverside 500 early in the year and went right on winning. At one point he won two races within 18 hours in Tennessee—the Smoky Mountain 200 at Maryville on a Saturday night and the Nashville 400 on a Sunday afternoon. His next victory, a 250-lapper on the quarter-mile asphalt oval at Bowman-Gray Stadium in Winston-Salem, North Carolina, gave him 100 Grand National victories. He wound up the year with ten victories and $109,000 in purses.

Then, in the 1970 Rebel 400 at Darlington, Petty nearly ended his career and his life. He lost control of his car coming out of the fourth turn. It ran up the concrete retaining wall, rode the wall awhile, then fell back onto the asphalt surface, flipped end over end, and then side over side before its spectacular journey ended in a heap of bent metal.

The 42,000 fans were stunned into silence as the 32-year-old star was carried unconscious from the car and hurried to the track hospital. Few felt he could survive such a savage smash-up. But a few minutes later Lee Petty came out of the hospital grinning, followed by Richard—on a stretcher, but smiling and waving to the crowd.

He escaped with a dislocated shoulder, chipped bones, and cuts and bruises on his face and neck. He said, "They say you never know what you really are as a driver until after your first bad wreck. Now we'll know about me."

Everyone knew in short order. He was racing again within a month, and two weeks after that he led all but five of 153 laps to win over the road course at Riverside in the Falstaff 400. Later he won the Dixie 500 at Atlanta and the Texas 500 to wind up his curtailed campaign with an incredible 18 victories and $138,000 in prizes.

The following year he won his third Daytona 500 by ten seconds ahead of teammate Buddy Baker, collecting a first prize of $48,000, the biggest of his career. Weaving through a series of wrecks two laps from the finish, he won the Carolina 500, his twelfth super-speedway victory, tying the record of Freddie Lorenzen. Then Richard raced on to set a new standard. In the American 500 at Rockingham, North Carolina, he led the last 143 laps to win by a full lap, for his 13th win. Then in the Dixie 500 at Atlanta he survived a stormy duel with Bobby Allison during the final 50 miles to take a thriller by five feet.

The Atlanta triumph boosted his career earnings to over a million dollars. A.J. Foyt was racing's only other "millionaire," and Richard was the first to attain that height strictly in stock cars. At the end of the year he had won 21 races, finished in the top five in 17 others, won $309,000 (a single-season record) and his third driving

In the lead at Michigan International Speedway, Petty (43) is drafted by one of his top competitors, David Pearson.

championship. The only other driver with three titles was Richard's father.

Characteristically, Richard played down his accomplishments. "We have come out pretty far ahead financially," he admitted. "Still, it's been a struggle, and I'm just a poor ol' country boy trying to keep my head above water."

The car-denting duel with Bobby Allison carried over into 1972. As the bitter rivals slugged it out on the track, observers feared that someone—Petty, Allison or an innocent bystander—might be killed. In one three-week period, the two top drivers banged into each other in three races, and Petty prevailed at the end of each.

Allison said, "He bumped me out of the first one, so I

bumped him trying to put him out of the second one. By the third one we were just doing what comes naturally. It's not good, but you can't let a guy get away with anything out there."

After the third duel, in the Wilkes 400, in which Petty and Allison rammed each other repeatedly, Richard's brother Maurice took some punches at Allison before others intervened. Richard said, "He was playing with my life out there. It made me mad and it scares me some. We can't go on this way."

They didn't. Their tempers cooled and their tactics grew less violent as the season wore on. But Petty had proven again that he was a cool customer who would not back down from a fight. "One thing about our racing," he said, "you can bend a little metal without breaking yourself up." Petty won his fourth driving title, breaking the last of his father's major records, despite the challenges of Bobby Allison and a growing number of talented young drivers.

For the 1973 season the Petty team accepted sponsorship support from Andy Granatelli's STP Corporation. Fat, flamboyant Andy, who had promoted his gasoline and oil additive into a million-dollar business, tried to talk Richard into repainting his cars STP red, but Petty insisted on keeping the familiar "Petty blue." He would only allow red STP stripes along the sides of the car. "I offered him fifty grand to repaint the entire car," said Granatelli, "but he refused."

Granatelli was pacified when Richard carried the STP emblem to victory in the Daytona 500. After Granatelli gave Richard a big (and unwanted) kiss in the victory circle, Richard grinned and said, "He sure loves that spotlight, but we can get along because I don't care for it much."

Although Richard was as unassuming as ever, he had changed his looks over the years. In 1973 he wore what he called "a riverboat gambler's long hair and sideburns and a gunfighter's mustache." The only other thing that changed was his bank account. By year's end he had won 154 Grand National races, including 22 super-speedway classics, and $1.5 million in purses, all records for his circuit.

And 1974 started sensationally when he survived fierce fighting among the leaders and track-littering wrecks to finish in front for the fifth time in the Daytona 500. No other driver had won more than once. Petty was leading 40 laps from the finish when his left front tire popped as he sped around the fourth turn. He kept his crippled car under control and steered right into the pits, where his crew replaced the rubber. Speeding out, he had fallen 37 second behind Bobby Allison's brother Donnie and seemed doomed. But he drove daringly and was closing in when Donnie's left front tire blew out with eleven laps left. Richard raced into the lead and took the checkered flag 25 miles later.

The season continued sensationally for Richard. He flashed home more than a lap in front in the Carolina 500 at Rockingham. In the Firecracker 400, he was driving right behind David Pearson at the beginning of the last lap, in position to slingshot around Pearson on the final straightaway. But Pearson slowed sharply on the first turn, and Richard had to pass to avoid hitting him. As they emerged from the final turn, it was Pearson who was able to shoot past Petty and win the race.

Richard and his wife Lynda wave to the crowds after Richard's fifth victory in the Daytona 500 in 1974.

Petty turned the tables on Pearson in the Talladega
500. This time he refused to pass until the last straight.
Then he bumped Pearson on the way by, and went on to
win by inches. Richard also won the Motor State 400, the
Dixie 500 and the Pocono 500 in Pennsylvania. Most of
the major races were reduced by 50 miles to conserve
fuel, but the paychecks were not cut, and Petty won more
than $250,000 for the season. He won five super-speed-
way races and only ten races in all, but clinched his fifth
driver title and the $75,000 bonus that went with it.

At the age of 37, Richard Petty was never far from the
front, and he was never reluctant to share the credit. One
day at Level Cross, wearing a sports shirt, Levis and high
boots, Richard observed, "Car racin' is a team sport. Pop
helps a lot. So does everyone around me. No driver ever
got to the finish line without a real good car around him.
You can't beat anyone walkin'. I help myself, too, more
than most drivers, because I work on my own cars more
than most, and so I know 'em better than most.
Otherwise, I just put my foot as far into it as I dare, I
steer and I try to stay out of trouble.

"We're goin' a lot faster. The cars are better so you
don't feel it, but it's riskier. We used to go 140 at the
fastest tracks, now we go 200. We used to run maybe two
or three 500-mile races a season. Now we run 20 or more.
The money's way up, of course. And money's nice. But I
got all I'll ever need."

He squinted into a setting sun. It was time for him to
return to work. He said, "We work eight or nine hours a
day, five or six days a week, just like anyone else. My
cousin puts the chassis together. My brother looks out for
the engines. I drive the cars. Mom watches over the
books, and pop watches over all of us. If I could make

more money running a supermarket, I'd run a super-market. It's a business, like any other business. Except it's more exciting.

"I love comin' home to the wife and kids in the country. And I love going racing in the big cities, and the small towns, too. Some teams pick their spots. We run 'em all.

"I don't know what I'll do when I can't race any more," he sighed, and for a second he seemed sad. But then he smiled and went back to work.

FIREBALL ROBERTS and JOE WEATHERLY

Excitement and Tragedy

If Lee Petty was the dominant stock car driver in the late 1950s and early '60s, he was not the most colorful or the most popular. He had plenty of competition from Buck Baker, who won the driving title in 1956 and '57, the Flock brothers and others.

But a new star was appearing on the horizon. He first gained attention in 1950 when he started in 63rd place in the first Southern 500 and finished second. By 1958, his black-and-gold Pontiac with its number 22 was the most familiar in the sport. The driver's name was Edward Glenn "Fireball" Roberts.

Roberts gained his nickname as a semi-pro fastball pitcher, but it seemed even more appropriate to his racing career. He worshiped speed and he worshiped winning. Curiously, some competitors in car racing do not care about speed. They drive only as fast as they have to go to win. The only lap they care about leading is the last one. But Roberts wanted to lead every lap. He drove like a demon, pushing his cars to their limit and often beyond. His hell-for-leather attitude may have lost him some races, but it also made him the most popular driver of his era.

Roberts drove with his head as well as his heart. He studied every track, learning where he could and could not pass, where he could take chances and where he had to drive conservatively. Then he went out and ran as fast as the track would bear. In qualifying heats he wanted the pole position every time, and in the race itself he wanted the lead—all the way.

Fireball won the pole position three years in a row in the Daytona 500 and was the fastest qualifier at Darlington's Southern 500 five times. He set speed records at every track he drove on—more records than any driver who ever raced. Although he held the lead in almost every race he ever entered, leading for 1,644 miles in Grand National races, his car often broke down before the finish. If he had ever found a flawless machine, Roberts might never have lost a race.

Roberts didn't care much about small races on small tracks. He was a glory guy who loved the spectaculars on the super-speedways. Still, he won 32 Grand National races and nine of those were super-speedway events.

During the late 1950s Fireball was the top driver on the well-supported Pontiac factory team. In 1957 he won the Rebel 300 at Darlington (then the only real super-track). In 1958 he came back to Darlington to win the Southern 500, and in 1959 he won the Rebel 300 again. That same year, he was the victor in the first Firecracker classic, run on the Fourth of July at the sparkling new super-oval at Daytona.

But after the 1960 season, Pontiac pulled out of racing and Roberts was left without a supporting factory team. Out of loyalty to Pontiac, he tried to race a car independently, but was shut out on the super-speedways in 1961. Convinced that factory support was necessary to win, Fireball reluctantly shifted to the Ford team. He was flooded with hate mail from Pontiac fans, but in 1962 he won the big Daytona 500 and was back in the winner's circle.

In 1963, the strong Ford team was challenged by a

Fireball Roberts poses in his car after winning the first Firecracker classic at Daytona in 1959.

spunky Chevrolet team led by driver Junior Johnson, another popular personality on the stock car trail. The Chevys won several races, and in the time trials for the Southern 500, Roberts was so eager to show them up that he pushed his car past its limits and slammed backwards into a wall.

While his car was being repaired and a new engine installed, Roberts watched Johnson lead the opening-day qualifiers at a speed of 133.4 miles per hour. The next day, Roberts' car was ready. He practiced during the damp early morning hours, then went out and surpassed Johnson's speed with an average run of 133.8 miles per hour. On race day, Roberts pushed Johnson for all he was worth. Finally Junior's car broke down and Fireball blazed on to win his second Southern 500.

Roberts had studied automotive engineering at the University of Florida, but dropped out after two years. He had already begun driving racing cars, running his first race in 1947 at the age of 18. Two years later he signed up for the new NASCAR circuit, and he gained the attention of the fans when he placed second in the Southern 500 at Darlington in 1950 at the ripe old age of 21.

Roberts didn't want to confine his driving to stock cars, either. He drove sports cars in the Daytona Beach 12-Hour Endurance race and the 24 Hours of LeMans in France. He also wanted very much to drive the Indianapolis 500, but at that time he would have had to leave NASCAR to run at Indy. NASCAR competition provided his main livelihood, so he was never able to do more than watch the big open-wheeled roadsters at Indianapolis.

In a car, Fireball Roberts was one of the most colorful

men on the circuit. Out of a car, he was colorless and withdrawn. He insisted on his privacy, avoiding the press and the public. He seemed at home only on the race track. He was comfortable only among other drivers, and was even a loner in that crowd. Although he was the first stock car driver to become famous outside of the South, he once said, "No one knows me very well." This was because he didn't let many know him.

Roberts was proud of his position. He considered himself a professional, and he sneered at amateurs. He considered an amateur anyone who put on a uniform and a helmet and called himself a driver without earning the title. He said that if you put up a track with an escape road in a tight turn, some amateurs might take the turn faster than pros, knowing they could take the escape road if they got into trouble. But if you set the same tight turn on a mile-high cliff without an escape, the amateur would slow down, but the pro would take it at the same speed.

"That's why fans pay to see races," he said. "They know the guy in the car is risking his neck."

Roberts was perhaps the flashiest and most exciting driver of his time. But many of the other daredevils lived wild lives off the tracks as well as on it. One of these men was Roberts' big competitor in 1962 and 1963. He was "Little Joe" Weatherly, a short, homely, curly-haired man, six years older than Fireball.

Little Joe started out driving motorcycles. As a boy he would drive through his hometown of Norfolk, Virginia, standing on the seat. "I got started on my 'cycle with the wilder type of boys," he once recalled. "We'd drive cross-country. I'd take the bike out on Friday afternoon and bring it back with the handlebars broke, the frame bent, a wheel twisted or an engine blown on Monday morning. I'd also have a few things broken on me. See this scar running from my left eye to my chin? It came on a street, not a track."

After he got three speeding tickets in one month and got his driver's license suspended, Weatherly decided that he ought to do his racing on tracks. By the time he had left motorcycles for stock cars, he had won the national 'cycle racing championship twice.

Then in the late 1950s, Little Joe Weatherly became a legend on the stock car circuit—not so much for the races he won as for the life he led. He would show up at the track in a gaudy sports shirt, black-and-white saddle shoes and golf gloves. He was an aggressive driver, but his off-the-track antics earned him the title "The Clown Prince of Racing."

One season he carried around a box, telling people there was a fierce mongoose inside. After he convinced someone, Joe would open the box and a piece of fur on a spring would jump out at the victim. One day Joe tried the trick on Bob Colvin, president of Darlington Raceway. Colvin was prepared—he pulled out a gun and began shooting wildly at the "mongoose" and at Little Joe. Joe turned and ran in terror before he realized Colvin was firing blanks.

Little Joe's best friend on the tour was Curtis "Pops" Turner. Turner was a great driver who also had a talent for investing his money. The two racers sometimes threw parties that lasted for days. During one of them, Little Joe drove a rented car into a motel swimming pool. Another time, Joe filled the water cooler in Turner's pit with mint juleps, the favorite alcoholic drink of Southern

Little Joe Weatherly takes the lead as he rounds one of the high-banked turns at Darlington.

gentlemen, then drove into Turner's pit during the race and asked for a swig himself.

Weatherly ran so hard off the track that he was winning few races on the track. But then in 1961 his friend Turner was suspended from all NASCAR events for trying to organize a drivers' union. With Turner gone, Little Joe got serious. He wanted to run every race on the circuit, and when his own car wasn't ready, he would turn up at the track and beg a ride from another team.

Nothing would stop him. In one race at Savannah, Georgia, his car went out of control, somersaulted six times, flew over a 20-foot fence and landed in a drainage ditch. Joe walked away from the wreckage. "All I got out of it was two bloodshot eyes," he laughed. Then he got into his own car and drove 685 miles to Moycock, North Carolina, where he competed in a race the next night. "If you want to cash in," he explained, "you've got to be there when the man puts his hand out with the money."

Little Joe won only 24 Grand National races in his career, and few of those were at super-speedways. But in 1962 and 1963 he ran so many races and placed in the top five so often that he won the driver's championship both years. He was 40 years old when he won the second title.

Then in January 1964 Little Joe entered the Riverside 500 in California, the only Grand National event run on

Weatherly (left) clowns for former driving great Jack Smith.

an irregular road course rather than an oval. During the week before the race he told a reporter, "Nothing comes easy to anyone in racing and certainly nothing ever came easy to me, but it's a great sport and now that I'm on top, all the struggles seem worthwhile."

Asked if he felt fear, he grinned and said, "Yes, but I don't let it get the upper hand of me. They build these cars pretty good, and the people who run the sport do everything they can to keep it safe. Shucks, you wouldn't want it too safe. What would be the fun of it then?" He confessed that while he wore a seat belt, he did not wear a shoulder harness because he got fidgety in the cockpit and liked to feel free to squirm around.

On race day, the throttle of Little Joe's car jammed as he traveled through a turn at 100 miles per hour. He slammed into a retaining wall in front of the bleachers with such force that grandstand patrons were showered with glass from his windshield. He was wrenched forward and killed by head injuries he suffered. He was 41 years old.

Little Joe's death shocked the stock car world. Although the drivers all knew that death and injuries might be just around the next turn, the loss of a particularly popular racer made them dwell on possibilities they usually tried not to think about. Fireball Roberts, for instance, had developed an ulcer, hiding his worries from the world. He once confided to a reporter, "When everything is working perfectly, I'm no more afraid than I am driving the family car on a highway. When something goes wrong, it scares the hell out of me. Something's always going wrong, but that's what makes it fun."

As time went on, however, Roberts spoke less and less about "fun." He admitted, "I get scared in racing. I'm always scared. What scares me most is fire."

Four months after Weatherly's death, Roberts entered the World 600 at Charlotte. Charlotte was his jinx track, the only one he had never conquered. He had won the pole position there five times and had finished second twice, but he never finished first. In the World 600, his car collided with those of Ned Jarrett and Junior Johnson, spun in the backstretch, flipped upside down, rammed rear-end first into a concrete retaining wall and exploded in flames.

Jarrett's car crashed in flames, too, but he leaped from it to run to Roberts. "My God, Ned, help me, I'm on fire," Roberts pleaded. Ned pulled Fireball from the inferno and beat the flames off his fireproof uniform with his bare hands.

Roberts was rushed to a hospital with severe burns over more than half of his body. He fought valiantly for 40 days. He seemed well on his way to recovery when he developed severe infections, then contracted pneumonia and died. It was ironic that a driver nicknamed "Fireball" should die in the aftermath of a fiery crash.

Roberts' death, coming two years after the retirement of Lee Petty and only a few months after the death of Little Joe Weatherly, ended an era in stock car racing. A few of the men who started with NASCAR in 1949 were still driving, but they were nearing retirement.

The stock car circuit was changing with the addition of super-speedways and the gradual move away from the short dirt tracks of the South. And much of the credit for the growth of the sport belonged to its early stars.

Fireball Roberts (22) and David Pearson (6) skid after a collision in the 1964 Atlanta 500. Later that season Roberts was severely burned in a crash at Charlotte and died of his injuries.

One of the younger racers, Ned Jarrett, summed up the contributions of Fireball Roberts. "Fireball was the most respected driver there ever was or maybe ever will be," he said. "He was the ideal. A lot of drivers copied him, but few had his ability. He had as much to do with making stock car racing the major sport it is today as anyone else in the world."

POPS TURNER and JUNIOR JOHNSON

Going Straight

Sports have provided a way for many boys who were going bad to go straight. Stock car racing was the road to a decent life for many, especially poor southern boys who would otherwise have spent their days making and selling illegal whiskey. Junior Johnson and Curtis "Pops" Turner were two who first learned to handle a car while making deliveries of illegal liquor, got in trouble with the law and found a respectable profession in racing.

As a young man Curtis Turner drove a fast Ford coupe with big springs in the back to handle heavy loads of bootleg whiskey. He knew the back roads like the back of his hand. Making deliveries on pitch-black nights, sometimes running faster than 100 miles per hour, he easily lost any law officers who spotted him, suspected his mission and took off after him.

"Some ol' state trooper ran me thirty-nine times, but

48

he never come close," Curtis once recalled. "I used to talk with that ol' trooper between times and he'd say, 'I'm gonna catch you with the goods if it's the last thing I do,' but he never did."

No one ever outran Turner, but the law finally caught up with him. "Before I knew better I used to steal some," he said. "Those was hard times back in the hills and you did things you shouldn't ought to have done to get by. But if you take what's not yours, you got to give something back sooner or later. I got caught and I got scared and I saw I had to go straight or wreck my life. I was wrong, and racing got me right. I'm not proud of my past, but I am proud of the future I made for myself."

Turner worked at the Little Creek Naval Station in Norfolk, Virginia, and he found a way to steal sugar from the Base. Sugar was necessary in making whiskey, so Turner would trade the sugar to bootleggers in return for whiskey. Then he would sell the illegal liquor to sailors around Norfolk and make a handsome profit.

Authorities at the Naval Station found out about Turner's thefts. They let him load up with 500 pounds of sugar and tried to arrest him on the way out of the gate. But he crashed the barricade and took off into the countryside with the police in pursuit.

His Ford flew through the suburbs, across the county line and into the foothills of the mountains, where he lost his pursuers. However, by then every law officer in the area had been alerted to look for him. He ran out of gas, siphoned some from a parked school bus and set out for home in Roanoke, Virginia. When he got there, the police were waiting for him.

Arrested and tried, he was fined $1,000, but a two-year jail sentence was suspended. On probation, he looked around for work but lacked the schooling to get a good job. Hearing that some of the boys were racing their cars Sunday afternoon in a cornfield near Mount Airy, North Carolina, he went to see what was happening and got hooked on racing. He was in his late 20s when he started his spectacular career.

Turner, who eventually picked up the nickname "Pops," started out driving on the backwoods dirt tracks throughout the South. Many were "outlaw" tracks, lacking the sanction of official racing groups and sometimes operating without the permission of local law enforcement authorities. Racing on such tracks was a risky business. There were few safety precautions, the races were loosely supervised, and the purses were small. No records of winners were kept or published, but Turner's reputation spread by word-of-mouth.

It is said that he won more than 350 races in his career, and stories circulated for years about the way he drove on the tiny dirt ovals. He would "broadslide" through the corners, always on the verge of losing control, and could almost always "outbrave" his opponents. He came up to NASCAR late in his career and won only 17 races, but his reputation had preceded him, and his popularity was far greater than his record suggests.

Turner won his first super-speedway race at Darlington in the Southern 500 in 1956. In 1958 he won the Rebel 300 there in a stirring stretch drive against his friend Little Joe Weatherly. He and Weatherly were famous for their high life off the track, but there were other interesting sides to Turner as well.

To begin with, Turner made a fortune investing in a lumber business and other ventures. He also invested a million dollars in the construction of a new super-speedway at Charlotte, North Carolina, and lost most of it. As soon as Pops made a fortune, he would promptly lose it.

"Easy come, easy go," he growled. "I've made a few fortunes, but I like to live good."

Turner could be amazingly generous—not only with his money but with his time and skills. Once he and some friends left a party to attend a minor league dirt track race in Richmond, Virginia. There are not many blacks in car racing even today, and there were even fewer in southern stock car racing in the 1950s—most southern whites were opposed to black participation. But this night

Curtis Turner smiles after running a modified stock car race at Daytona in 1952. He was still four years from winning a Grand National event.

Standing on the hood of his car, Turner accepts the cheers of the crowd and the winner's trophy after a big victory at Darlington.

Turner noticed a black team struggling with what seemed to him the worst-looking race car he'd ever seen.

"I believe somebody needs some help," he said. In his fancy clothes, he jumped the fence and went into the pits. Without telling them who he was, he went to work on their car. He got the engine running so well that when the race was called the team let him take the car out and he jumped in the driver's seat. He won the race, received the winner's check, turned it over to the team and disappeared into the night. The next week, when another driver asked if he could drive their car, the black owners were firm. "No, sir," one said, "this car is reserved for the big man in the white shirt and fancy cuff links."

Turner finally got into trouble with NASCAR boss Bill France, and it seemed his racing career on the major stock car circuit was over. Turner became friendly with representatives of the Teamsters' Union and agreed to try to organize a union for race drivers. His efforts failed, but Bill France was angry enough to suspend Turner indefinitely in 1961. Pops went back to rebuilding his fortune and occasionally raced on outlaw tracks, but NASCAR fans missed the color and excitement he brought to the sport.

At the time Turner was suspended, the talk of auto racing was a new driving technique called "drafting," which was bringing new excitement to the tracks. The discoverer of the new trick was a driver named Junior Johnson. He was seven years younger than Pops Turner, but he had come from much the same background— whiskey-running.

Johnson was born in Ronda, North Carolina, in 1931. He was a left-handed pitcher on his school baseball team.

Although he was a regular at the local Baptist Church, which frowns on alcoholic beverages, he got caught up in being a delivery boy in the bootlegging business before he was out of his teens. He once said, "It's nothin' to be proud of, but it's something I had to do before I found something smarter and better to do.

"I'd say nearly everybody in a fifty-mile radius of here was in the whiskey business at one time or another," he recalled. "When we grew up here, everybody seemed to be more or less messin' with whiskey, and myself and my two brothers did quite a bit of transportin'. During the depression here, people either had to do that or starve to death. It wasn't no gangster type of business or nothin'. Gettin' caught and pullin' time, that was just part of it. Me and my brothers, when we went out on the road at night, it was just like a milk run, far as we were concerned."

Starting about midnight, the "milk deliveries" began. In order to deliver the whiskey to the buyers and avoid getting caught, a man needed a hot car, knowledge of the back roads and plenty of driving skill. Junior had all three. "There wasn't no way you could make my car sound like an ordinary car," he said. So he sacrificed secrecy for speed, and roared through the nights, waking up sleeping citizens in back country cabins.

If he ran into a road block set up by Alcohol Tax Division agents, Junior would hold the accelerator to the floorboard while slamming on the brakes, spin the steering wheel and skid into a screaming about-face. Then he would head right back where he'd come from.

In his early 20s, Johnson started racing on local tracks, but he kept up the family whiskey business. Then one day agents spotted his still and arrested him. Johnson

served ten months at the federal reformatory in Chilli-
cothe, Ohio. When he got out he went back to racing,
seeing it as a way for him to go straight and earn a decent
legal living. He joined the Grand National tour in a race
at Hickory, North Carolina, in 1954 and finished fifth in
a Hudson.

He had a lot to learn, but he didn't discourage easily.
For a few years, victories were scarce. If he won five or
six small races in a season, it was a good year. Three
times he broke into the top ten in the final driving
standings. Gradually he started to concentrate on the big
super-speedway races, and within a few years he became
"the man to beat." By the time he retired, he had won 50
Grand National races, then the third most of all time.
Eight of his victories were on the super-speedways.

Surprisingly, Johnson never finished in the top five in
the driver standings. He didn't pile up points because if
he couldn't finish first he didn't care if he finished. He
said, "Second place is no place." He was a charger who
took chances others would not take. He pushed his cars
until they broke. He ran ahead in many races that he
later lost because he never could compete conservatively.

He said, "You put your car in front of everybody else
and keep it there as long as it'll hold together. You drive
through a fence if you have to get to that finish line first."
One time he did crash through a fence. He spun his car
into an about-face and drove right back through the hole
in the fence, back onto the track and back into the race.
He said, "I don't know how you can win a race if you're
not in the lead."

It was ironic that a charger like Junior Johnson
discovered "drafting," a new racing trick that gave the
advantage to the car running behind. But for Junior it

Junior Johnson supervises the replacement of an engine in one of his cars after his 1966 retirement as a driver.

was an invention born of necessity. It was February 1960. Junior still had not won a major race and he seemed unlikely to win this one—the Daytona 500. He was driving a Chevy that was outclassed that year by Pontiacs, Fords and Plymouths.

In the qualifying heats, Fireball Roberts had put his Pontiac on the pole at better than 151 miles per hour. Jack Smith, Cotton Owens and Bobby Johns put other Pontiacs in the next three starting spots. Freddie Lorenzen and Joe Weatherly qualified Fords fifth and seventh. Jim Reed got a Chevy in sixth and Rex White got one in eighth, while Johnson settled for ninth. Farther back in the field were the Petty Plymouths.

Johnson was disgusted, but not discouraged. He had come up with an idea in practice. "In the preliminary races, the warm-ups and stuff like that, they was smoking me off the track," he recalled. "I went out for a practice run, and Fireball Roberts was out there in a Pontiac. I got in right behind him on a curve, right on his bumper. I knew I couldn't stay with him on the straightaway. But as I came out of the curve right behind him, I noticed a funny thing: as long as I stayed right in behind him, I noticed I picked up speed and my car was going faster than it had ever gone before. It felt like the car was plumb off the ground and just floating along."

He learned that if a driver is willing to put his car right behind the car ahead of him, the vacuum created by the front car will suck the back car along. By "drafting," as the technique came to be known, a slower car could stay right with the leader without running as hard.

And Johnson discovered something even more amazing. When a drafting car swings out to pass the lead car, the vacuum pulls it forward for a split second, producing a sling-shot effect, allowing the drafting car to shoot past the leader. Both discoveries had historic significance, although no one knew it then.

Race day that February was filled with excitement. Daytona was the biggest and newest track in the sport, and this was only the second running of the Daytona 500. Fireball Roberts was the favorite, and he roared out to the lead as the green flag was unfurled and the big, gaudy cars started to speed around the steeply banked track. But Roberts' car faded fast, and Jack Smith shot into the lead. Then Lee Petty, who had worked his way through the tight tangle of traffic, went in front.

Fans began to notice that Johnson was driving very close to the cars in front of him. Many wondered why he was driving so dangerously. Still, he leaped into the lead for a while early in the race before dropping back again.

Tiger Tom Pistone went ahead, then Rex White. But Johnson continued to "hitch rides" on cars in front of him, sticking to their tails as if he were pasted there. If they slowed suddenly, of course, there would be a pile-up, but Johnson was willing to run that risk. It was the only way his slow car could keep up with the others.

Near the halfway point, Johnson jumped back in front again. Again, he was unable to keep the lead, but at 400 miles he remained in contention, tagging behind every fast car he could get close to. Bobby Johns came up to challenge the Pettys, and Johnson went with him, glued to his rear bumper. Johnson stayed right near the front as the cars ate up the last laps. By now the fans were shouting for him, admiring his daring tactics, even if they didn't understand the "lift" he was getting from other cars.

With ten laps of the 200-lap marathon remaining, wind pressure sucked the rear window from Bobby Johns's car. The shock of it spun him out of control for a second, and Johnson swung around him and into the lead. Before Johns could get straight and set out in pursuit, Johnson was far in front. Johns closed the gap, but he couldn't catch Junior.

After four-and-a-half hours of tough, tactical competition, Junior Johnson sped under the checkered flag to record his first major victory with Johns and the Pettys close behind. During a wild scene in Victory Lane, someone said to him, "Hey, boy, you did something different."

Johnson grinned and said, "I jus' did what I could do."

Junior Johnson's edge did not last long. At first, others were afraid to try the tricky tactic, but soon all the drivers were doing it. Drafting tightened competition, closing the gap between faster and slower cars, and it led to closer finishes than in any other type of racing.

After Johnson's big win at Daytona he stayed near the top. If his car was fast enough, he led as long as the car lasted. If it was slower, he drafted faster cars to keep up. In 1962 he won the National 500 at Charlotte and nearly won the Southern 500 at Darlington. (Officials announced eight hours after the race that there had been a scoring error and Larry Frank had won instead.)

In 1963, factory-backed Fords were the fastest cars on the circuit. Junior Johnson was still running Chevys, and without the money or the equipment of the Ford team, he gave the favorites quite a battle. The press and public really supported Johnson's efforts, and he repaid them by winning the Dixie 400 at Atlanta and the National 400 at

Johnson stays a car-length ahead of Richard Petty in the 1962 Southern 500. His slogan was said to be, "We lead, others follow."

Charlotte, as well as six other races. He would have won the World 600 at Charlotte had he not run out of fuel with just five miles left.

The 1964 season was darkened by the deaths of Fireball Roberts and Joe Weatherly. The tragedies jarred Junior Johnson, and he began to consider retirement. But he kept running. In 1965 he won six straight races, including the Rebel 300 at Darlington. It was his last big victory. In 1966 he hung up his driving uniform for the last time. Only in his mid-30s, he seemed older.

He said, "They're running right on the ragged edge now. They're goin' so fast, you don't drive 'em, you aim 'em. I've always been a charger and I don't want to race any other way, but they're going too fast for me. I just don't feel I can go as hard as I could a year ago or the year before that.

"Oh, I don't want to say I'm too old to drive or afraid to drive, but I jus' think it's time I stepped aside to let some young guys through. It's their turn now. I'll help 'em all I can."

As one relative youngster was retiring, an oldster was returning. Pops Turner, suspended by NASCAR in 1961, was reinstated for the 1965 season. Turner had been struck hard by the death of his friend Joe Weatherly the year before, and most fans felt that he would not even try a comeback. But the crafty old veteran fooled them. He confided to friends that he wanted to win a big one for Little Joe. So he resumed racing, working his way back toward the top.

Turner almost got his big one in the National 400 at Charlotte. Dueling for the lead, he crashed and suffered several cracked ribs, a particularly painful injury. Still, his car was not badly damaged. He got it back to the pits, got quick repairs and rejoined the race. At the finish he was only three car-lengths behind Freddie Lorenzen.

The next week, with his midsection taped up, Pops limped into the new North Carolina Motor Speedway in Rockingham for the inaugural race there, the American 500. In time trials, Turner eased gingerly into the cockpit, qualified safely and got out. He went to his garage, curled up on a bench and slept while Richard Petty and a couple of others ran faster.

On race day, Petty pulled away in the early going, but Turner kept within reach of the leaders. Junior Johnson took the lead, then David Pearson banged into Petty and finished his chances. At 100 laps, everyone was startled

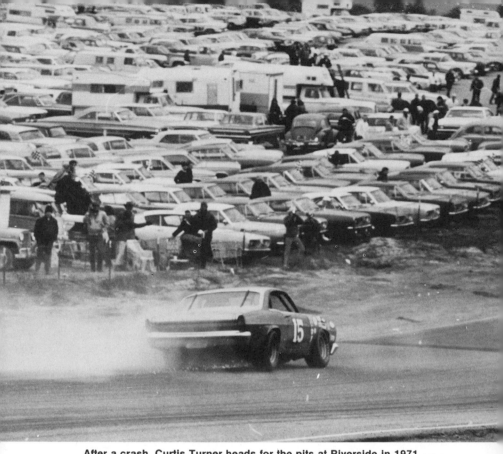

After a crash, Curtis Turner heads for the pits at Riverside in 1971 . . .

when Pops Turner took the lead, but 400 laps of the grueling grind on this one-mile oval remained.

Turner led 45 straight laps, then fell back. He charged to the front again on the 176th lap. At the halfway point, he was far in front, but tiring. Cale Yarborough and Richard Petty, driving relief for Jim Paschal, started to close in as the long race spun on.

Turner was in terrible pain. Petty passed him and pulled far in front of him, but Turner hung on. Then at 350 laps, the engine in Petty's car went sour; he slowed and went into the pits. Curtis Turner charged back in

. . . and his left front wheel almost gets there first.

front, and the crowd stood and cheered happily for the grand old guy.

Yarborough caught him on lap 439 and hung on for a long time, but Turner stayed right behind him. Turner caught up on lap 473 when Yarborough had to dart into the pits to replace his tires. Pops did not dare to pit now. The fans stood and screamed throughout the last laps as Cale pulled closer and closer to Pops.

Pops never went into the pits. He kept waiting for a tire to blow out, but it didn't. He feared he'd run out of fuel, but he didn't. Cale couldn't catch him, and Pops' Ford flew past the checkered flag in front. The ovation he received was enormous.

Asked if he would celebrate, Pops, worn out and wincing from the pain in his chest, smiled and said, "Well, I see no reason why we shouldn't start a brand new party. Everyone's invited. Little Joe would have liked that." And later, he added, "When I die, I want everyone to start one last party on me."

That was his last big victory. Two years later, at the advanced age of 43, he became the first driver to crack the 180-miles-per-hour barrier at Daytona to win the pole position for the 500. But he crashed in the race, and was lucky to escape serious injury. His racing days were about done.

Turner was a daredevil in the air as well as on the ground. He had flown his own light plane so wildly he was always in trouble with authorities. Several times he landed his plane on track straightaways. Once he landed it at a small-town shopping center to let out a friend.

In October of 1970 Pops was piloting his plane on his way to the Charlotte track when it crashed and he was killed. He was 46. By that time, the last of the old guard racers was gone. The newer drivers were mostly Southerners, but many were better educated and more sophisticated. Some came from the North—Indy star A.J. Foyt, Freddie Lorenzen and others. Times had changed, and the drivers were changing with them.

But no one had lived at a faster pace and given more excitement to the people of their region than the early NASCAR drivers. When Pops Turner died, his fellow racer Lee Petty had the last word: "He crammed about 76 years of living into his 46 years."

FREDDIE LORENZEN

The Carpetbagger

Fred Lorenzen was born in December of 1934 in Elmhurst, Illinois, and grew up in Chicago. His father was an electrical engineer and Freddie, who was good at working with his hands, at first thought he would become a carpenter.

But Freddie had another consuming interest—car racing. Most kids in Chicago who were race fans followed the Indianapolis racers—the big open-wheeled roadsters that competed for the United States Auto Club. But Freddie became entranced with the cars and drivers on the stock car circuit. He listened to the radio broadcasts of southern stock car races and sought out minor league stock car competition around Chicago.

"I heard all about Fireball Roberts, Joe Weatherly and Curtis Turner, and they were big heroes," he explained once. "I used to dream about Darlington and wonder what it would be like to win the Southern 500 there.

"When I was still pretty young, I got my hands on a midget car and I used to wheel it around the neighborhood pretty fast until the cops took it away from me. When I was sixteen, I started carpentering with my brother-in-law and joined the union. But I still dreamed of racing. A friend sold me a race car, a jalopy. I took it racing and rolled it over. But I was on my way."

He had a long way to go. His parents disapproved of racing, but Freddie raced anyway. In 1955 he drove hot rods at Soldier Field with some success. In 1956, at 22, he went south with all the money he could beg or borrow, hoping to race. He couldn't get rides at all for many races and got into only seven events. After winning only $235 all year, he finally went home to Chicago flat broke.

Lorenzen drove in NASCAR's minor league events in the East and Midwest in 1957. Then he switched to USAC's midwestern stock car circuit in 1958 and 1959. He began to get good cars, and he began to win races in a hurry, capturing the USAC stock car driving titles both years. He was proving he had the ability, but he was still suffering financially. "The best year I had, I won $14,000, a trophy and a gold watch," he grinned. It was hardly enough to pay his expenses, so in 1960 he switched back to NASCAR to take another crack at Grand National competition.

This time he took his own car south, prepared it and drove it himself. He soon discovered that an independent operator could hardly compete against the well-financed racing teams. He failed to win a race in 1960, earning only $8,000 in prizes and spending much more than that.

"I slept in the back seat of my car and ate peanut butter sandwiches half the time," he recalled. "It didn't pay off. I really got discouraged this time. I owed

Young Freddie Lorenzen dries off after winning a 250-mile race in Milwaukee on the United States Auto Club circuit in 1959.

$10,000. I sold my car and trailer for $7,500, paid off $4,500 of my debts, quit racing and went home to earn the rest. I was going to go to work as a carpenter, forget racing and just try to bail myself out of hock."

Then Ralph Moody called and asked Lorenzen to drive a new Ford for the Holman-Moody team. John Holman and Ralph Moody had put together a tremendously talented racing organization. They had factory support from Ford and were able to put top equipment on the track. Needing a skilled, tough young driver, they decided to gamble on Lorenzen.

"I was surprised, but thrilled," Lorenzen recalled. "Just knowing they'd seen enough in me to want me to drive for them boosted my morale way back up. I had confidence I could win in their cars. I forgot all about retiring. I knew I'd have to hammer a lot of nails to square myself. Now one big win would wipe out all my debts."

He got his first big victory at Darlington in the 1961 Rebel 300. Darlington is the toughest track in top car racing circles. At one and three-eighths miles, it is shorter than other super-speedways and has tighter turns. It wasn't built with high banks like the other big-time raceways. The track is narrow and irregular, so that a driver can only pass safely in a few places. The back-stretch is fast, but a car must be right up against the guard rail going into the third turn to cut the corner correctly. Drivers often get so close that they scrape the paint off the right sides of their cars. This scrape has come to be known as the "Darlington Stripe."

Freddie Lorenzen picked up his "Darlington Stripe" during the Rebel 300 trying to get around Curtis Turner. It was late in the race, they were running for the lead and Pops was making it almost impossible for Freddie to pass him. One time Lorenzen tried to duck past on the inside and Turner drove down low to cut him off. A lap later, Lorenzen tried to sweep by above him and Turner swung so wide he almost ran Freddie into the wall. Finally, with two laps left, Lorenzen went high. As Pops swung wide again, Freddie cut sharply to the low side and flew by the startled Turner on the inside.

Ralph Moody later recalled, "Watching him try to get by, I knew Freddie had come to the time he had to prove himself as a race driver. When he used his head and a lot of guts to get by the old guy, he proved himself to me."

Lorenzen agreed. "I felt it was a sort of a test, too," he said. "I passed it, and I felt good about it. I didn't want anything to be given to me."

Moments after Freddie took the lead, Turner tried to repass him, and Freddie used the same tactics Turner had. Lorenzen went on to win the race and the admiration of his rivals.

"There are a lot more Northerners in NASCAR Grand National racing now than there were then," Lorenzen said years later. "I was considered something of a carpetbagger, coming down to cash in on their circuit. I didn't talk their language. I couldn't even understand their southern slang and their southern accents at first. But they're a good bunch of guys. Race drivers are race drivers. Once I proved myself to them, they accepted me as one of them."

One way he proved himself was with the sort of courage that caused him to be called "Fearless Freddie." One year he won the Old Dominion 500 without brakes. In 1964 he came upon a wreck, slid into the infield grass and was rammed by another car. He was hospitalized with two cracked bones in his back and severed tendons in a wrist. But two days later he ducked out of the hospital to serve as a pallbearer at Fireball Roberts' funeral. He won his first race on his return, a 500-lapper in lethal heat, with his back strapped in a brace.

If Lorenzen had the lead in a race, he wouldn't move over for anyone. In a race at Atlanta he blocked off Junior Johnson and Junior was furious. He drawled, "He sort of swerves and fishtails right in front of me, tryin' to keep me from goin' round him. If he ain't agonna get outta my way, I'll jus' bore straight through him. If he ever does it again, I'll knock hell out of him."

Lorenzen laughed and kept on driving his way, and neither Johnson nor anyone else ever did him in.

Lorenzen's purses came to almost $30,000 in 1961. By agreement with Holman and Moody, Fred kept 40 percent of his winnings. He paid off his debts and opened a bank account. In 1962 he won only two races, but one was the lucrative Atlanta 500, and his earnings passed $40,000.

In 1963 he struck gold. He won six races, including the Atlanta 500 and the World 600. The World was worth almost $28,000, the top purse of his career. With prizes of

Lorenzen shows the spare, reinforced interior of his car before a race at Daytona. The chart on the dashboard converts laps into miles.

$113,750, he became the first driver to earn more than $100,000 in a single season.

In 1964 he won eight of sixteen races and earned $72,000. He earned $77,000 the following year. Business was booming and he was the star of the tour. He was regarded as "The Golden Boy."

Lorenzen was a perfectionist. By concentrating on the big tracks, he learned them well. He usually ran fewer than 20 races a year, and by keeping his cars off the small tracks, he kept them in good shape. He was not a charger. He would lay back, waiting for the right moment to move. He kept close to the leaders and was the ultimate master at drafting. When it was time to go for the lead, he went. The only lap he cared about leading was the last one. Time and again he won races when the

During the 1965 running of the Daytona 500, Lorenzen (28) roars by Junior Johnson on his way to a big win.

engines of the leaders broke down, earning the nickname "Lucky Lorenzen." However, he had his share of hard luck, too. Often he was the driver who had the race won when his engine went bad.

There was more than luck to Freddie's success. He kept his cars in one piece and in contention. He was ready to take advantage of every opportunity that presented itself to him.

In the National 500 at Charlotte in 1965, he saw that he had to run with A.J. Foyt or Foyt would run away from him. Foyt was Fred's best friend in racing, but Fred would not give Foyt the slightest advantage on the track. They ran almost bumper to bumper for 100 miles. Then when they got high into a turn together, neither would back down. Fred was on the inside, and he drifted so high he drove Foyt into the outside wall. A.J. was out of the race and Freddie went on to win. "It was one of those things which happen in racing when you're running hard," Lorenzen sighed later.

In the World 600 at Charlotte in 1965, Lorenzen led twice in the early stages but then dropped back a bit to conserve his car while others fought for the lead. One by one the leaders dropped out, and Lorenzen fell into the lead. With 100 laps (150 miles) to go, he was three laps in front of Earl Balmer. Few cars remained in the running, and most of the stars had dropped out.

Now, however, Lorenzen started to lose power. His engine was weakening, and he was using enormous amounts of fuel. He had to pit repeatedly to replenish his fuel supply. Each time he did, he lost ground to Balmer. Able to run much faster, Balmer roared by Lorenzen once, then twice. Suddenly, he was in the same lap with the leader and closing in.

The spectacular stretch run had the crowd roaring. Freddie tried to wait for slowdown periods under the yellow flag when he could make a pit stop without losing so much ground to Balmer. But still Balmer kept closing the gap. Balmer was within a half-lap, then within a quarter-lap of the lead. Seeing Balmer right behind him, Lorenzen ignored orders from his pits to replace a worn tire and went on.

Balmer finally caught up. Then, trying to pass, he lost control of his car and scraped the guard rail in the third turn. He bounced off almost out of control, but he held on and set off after Lorenzen again.

With four laps left, Lorenzen led by four seconds. With three laps left, his lead was down to three seconds. With two laps left, it was only two seconds. Balmer was booming in on him, and the big crowd was standing and cheering the action.

Lorenzen came up on slower traffic in front of him and started to pick his way carefully through the also-rans, passing one high, another low. He was skilled at this, and he wasted no time. He made just the right moves and soon was clear. Balmer lacked Lorenzen's experience and ability. Passing a car which drifted high, Balmer swerved wildly. He saved himself from spinning out but lost four precious seconds.

On the last lap, Balmer bore in on Lorenzen again. He closed to within four seconds, three, two, one. He pulled within one car length of the leader. But Lorenzen hung on grimly, using up the whole track, offering no opening for the youngster to get by. As they came off the final turn, Lorenzen jammed his foot to the floorboard and pulled away from Balmer to win by three lengths.

Lorenzen had used everything his car had left, but he

had won the battle of wits and bravery. Later he said, "I wasn't about to outrun everybody for 580 or 590 miles and then blow it. I was out there adding up my money when I saw him coming at me. I forgot about the money and started to race all over again. It was a hard race, but I ran it right."

Freddie gave lots of credit to the team he raced for. "The car is the most important thing," he said. "There's a difference in drivers, but no one wins many races without having one of the best cars. That makes your owners and mechanics important. I've got the best behind me. Some guys say this is why I win. Sure, I can run an engine in practice hard; and if it blows, my team will pull another off the truck for me. The independents can't do this. I know that. I went that way, myself. And I lost."

But the tough, husky driver also took some credit for himself: "A lot of guys have my ability, but not many have my desire. You've got to have ambition and determination to get ahead, and you've got to be willing to make any sacrifices it takes. You need experience, too. You have to know how to plan a race according to the competition and how to adjust the plan as the race develops. Finally, you have to have guts. We lay our lives on the line. You crash and you get scared. Your friends get hurt or killed and you get depressed. You have to have the sort of hardness to live with that."

Lorenzen was basically a conservative driver, and he lived a conservative, clean-cut life off the track. A handsome bachelor, he dated a lot and lived well, but he was careful with his cash. "I've been broke, and I didn't like it," he explained. "I invest my money to protect my future. I drink a little beer, but no hard liquor. I don't smoke. I'll marry only after I retire."

Lorenzen waves to his fans after announcing his retirement in 1967.

Freddie won his last big race, the American 500 at Rockingham in 1966. Then he retired in 1967 and went home to Chicago. However, he lost some money in stock market reversals, found he missed racing and returned in 1970 after three years away.

Three years later, he retired again without winning another race. He may have lost his touch. Or maybe he just couldn't get the good rides again. He did make more than $45,000 in 1971, but he was struggling all the time. In the Southern 500 at Darlington, his car climbed the homestretch wall, wiped out twelve feet of it, veered off and cut down a telephone pole before spinning to a stop. Freddie suffered a brain concussion and cuts on his face and neck. His left foot was fractured so severely that it required surgery. He recovered and returned to racing the following season, earning $20,000, but it was no use. He retired, got married and settled down.

The carpetbagger from the North had proven himself in stock car racing. He won eleven super-speedway events and earned more than $400,000 in prize money. Most important, he had earned the respect of the southern crowds and drivers. Richard Petty once said that of all the drivers he faced on the super-speedway tracks, Freddie Lorenzen was the toughest, a tribute to Freddie's skill and determination.

A. J. FOYT

Invader from Indy

It was the worst year in car racing history, 1964. Eddie Sachs and Dave MacDonald had been killed in a flaming wreck early in the Indianapolis 500. Joe Weatherly had died at Riverside and Fireball Roberts in a fiery crash at Charlotte in NASCAR competition.

Still, the annual Fourth of July classic at Daytona, the Firecracker 400, had many fine drivers that year. Richard Petty, the leading driver on tour, was well on his way to his first Grand National driving title. Freddie Lorenzen was sizzling on the super-speedways, having already won about half his starts on this circuit. And there were several other seasoned stock car drivers who had to be considered outstanding contenders in every race.

Also at Daytona to drive in the Firecracker was a famous outsider. A.J. Foyt, who had won his second Indy 500 on Memorial Day, was visiting the NASCAR circuit, and he had come to win.

No Indianapolis champ ever had won a NASCAR classic, and few had dared to challenge the masters of the super-speedways. But Foyt had unsurpassed skill in any kind of car. The tough, temperamental Texan was 29, at the very peak of his prowess.

Five weeks earlier he had driven a Ford-engined car to victory at Indianapolis, and Ford had provided a stock car for the Firecracker. But A.J. couldn't make it run the way he wanted and went looking for a better car. He cared more about winning than about contracts and was determined to find a machine he thought he could win with. The manufacturers of Dodge, which had never won a super-speedway event and wanted badly to break through, came up with a car Foyt liked.

Petty's Plymouth was favored, and the Fords of Freddie Lorenzen and Junior Johnson as well as a Mercury driven by Darel Dieringer were regarded as the chief contenders. The Dodges driven by Foyt and stock car veteran Bobby Isaac were regarded as long shots.

In the time trials, Dieringer had the fastest early time, gaining the pole position. Then a rainstorm forced cancellation of the rest of the trials and most drivers had to gain starting positions in a 50-mile qualifying sprint the day before the big race.

Paul Goldsmith was leading the sprint when his Plymouth slid on an oil slick and spun wildly just as others roared toward him. Freddie Lorenzen braked hard, but spun into Goldsmith, setting off a chain of spinning crashes which involved both Foyt in his Dodge and Johnny Rutherford in the Ford Foyt had been scheduled to drive. Lorenzen was injured badly enough to miss the next day's race. The others were unhurt, but

Foyt's Dodge was damaged and he had to settle for the 19th starting position in the Firecracker.

On race day, a huge crowd listened to marching bands and watched speedboats skid across the infield lake before the race started. The cars were pushed into position, then the announcer asked for a moment of silence in memory of Fireball Roberts, who had won this race three times. Then came the command to start the engines. The big, beautiful cars roared to life and started to circle the oval in position behind the pace car.

As the green flag flew, Dieringer darted to the front. But almost immediately, back in the bunch, a tire blew on Reb Wickersham's Pontiac. The car careened into the homestretch wall and rebounded into the path of the oncoming racers, right in front of Foyt's Dodge. Reacting instantly, Foyt wrestled his hurtling car around his wrecked rival, missing him by inches.

Richard Petty caught and passed Dieringer and was in front as the cars streamed across the start-finish line the first time. Petty had the fastest car in the field and a clear track in front of him for a while, and at 170 miles per hour he easily pulled away from his rivals. Meanwhile, Foyt, driving daringly, was working his way through traffic, passing cars on every lap.

At 10 laps, Foyt was in 15th place. At 15 laps, he was 10th. At 20 laps, he was 5th. He handled the big stock cars as well as he handled the lightweight Indy cars that were more familiar to him. To him, a race car was a race car.

Foyt had spotted Petty a tremendous edge in this race, however, and Richard was running away from him out front. After 250 miles (100 laps on the two-and-a-half-

mile track), with 150 miles to go, Petty was almost a lap
in the lead, but Foyt and Bobby Isaac were swapping
second place back and forth and starting to pose a threat
to the leader.

At 103 laps, a Dodge driven by Ken Spikes slammed
into the fence on the fourth turn, skidded off and flipped
upside down in the infield. While the fans were watching
his wild ride, few noticed Petty's power plant give way.
With a puff of smoke, his engine broke and Richard
steered his crippled Plymouth into the pits, finished for
the day.

Foyt saw it as he flew past and into the lead, closely
pressed by Isaac. Suddenly the race was between two red
Dodges. Isaac had the faster car, but Foyt could outdrive
him in the turns.

Foyt led, then Isaac, then Foyt again, then Isaac again. Isaac knew all the tricks of the super-speedways, and he was using every one to hold off Foyt. But A.J. was learning fast. Foyt slipped by Isaac on lap 156, but then Isaac regained the lead two laps later with only two laps left. By now the crowd was on its feet and cheering.

As the cars entered the final lap, Foyt was pressing Isaac, seeking a way around him. On the backstretch, Foyt drove daringly low, slipped inside Isaac and drew even with him. Through the third turn, Foyt pulled in front. The two cars blazed down the short chute and into the fourth corner. Foyt came out of it a car length in the lead.

As they sped into the homestretch, Isaac went wide and drew alongside Foyt on the outside. As the cars

His car patched from the time trial accident, A.J. Foyt (47) roars toward the finish of the 1964 Firecracker 400, pursued by three rivals.

After the '64 Firecracker, A.J. accepts the trophy for his first big victory in NASCAR competition.

rocketed toward the finish line, they were almost even. Foyt pressed the accelerator to the floorboard. Isaac could not catch him. As they came home under the checkered flag, Foyt had his car inches in front.

Even as an outsider, Foyt was hailed as a hero. The fans recognized his ability and bravery. His sweat-stained, grease-smeared face broke out in a broad grin as he accepted congratulations and the title trophy in Victory Lane.

He had done it for Dodge, but more for himself. This was his first Grand National triumph, but it would not be his last. He inspired a series of challenges by Indianapolis drivers in NASCAR classics, some of which paid off handsomely. Dan Gurney, Parnelli Jones, Mark Donohue, Mario Andretti and Jim Hurtubise all won major NASCAR events in the next few years.

On his home grounds or on foreign territory, Foyt could beat the best. In stock car classics, no one ever won more races in fewer starts. Racing only when the stock car events did not compete with championship races of the United States Auto Club (USAC), A.J. proved his versatility. Richard Petty observed, "There is no one I admire more or like to race less than Foyt. He comes down here and picks our pockets. But he is a real racer and you have to respect him. There is no one I ever wanted to whip more."

Anthony Joseph Foyt, Jr., was born January 16, 1935, in Houston, Texas. His father, a former race driver and mechanic, ran a garage. When A.J. was three years old, his father gave him a blood-red miniature racer. "I thought that little ol' car was the most beautiful thing there ever was," Foyt recalled.

A.J. took to the car as if he had been born in it. When he was six, he was driving it in exhibitions between races at a local track. When he was eleven and his parents were away at a race, he got their midget car out of their garage and ran it in the backyard until it caught fire. He bailed out, put out the fire and went to bed.

At 17, Foyt quit school and began to race motorcycles. Then he raced jalopies and stock cars on the dusty, dangerous, bush-league back-tracks of the Southwest. He won in everything he raced. He moved up to midget cars and sprint cars, which are smaller versions of Indianapolis cars, and to the better tracks of the Midwest.

Every year he scraped up the money to go to Indianapolis for the 500. Then in 1958 he qualified to start the race himself. At 25, he was the youngest driver in the starting field. In 1960 he won his first race on the USAC championship trail, a series of major races for Indy-type cars. Then he won four of the last six events on the tour and his first USAC driving title. The following year he won the Indianapolis 500 in a spectacular race with Eddie Sachs and went on to win the driving crown a second time. In 1963 he lost a wheel during the Indy 500, putting him out of the race, but he won his third driving championship.

In 1964 Foyt won a record ten races on the USAC championship trail, his second Indianapolis 500 and his fourth driving title. His ten victories were roughly the equivalent of winning ten super speedway-classics in stock car racing in a single season. He also won that Firecracker 400 at Daytona, his first NASCAR super-speedway classic.

He was a remarkable racer. Driver Parnelli Jones said,

"I think I succeeded in racing because I had more determination than most drivers. But Foyt had more than I had, more than anyone else ever had. I would do almost anything to win a race. Foyt would do anything."

Foyt said of himself, "I could never settle for being anything but the best. I could never stand to be second."

He drove the small races as hard as he drove the big ones. Several times when his car went bad during pre-race trials, he bought his way into starting fields. Once he paid a driver for the right to drive a car which had qualified to start dead last in a short, unimportant race. A.J. drove like a demon to win. It wasn't the small purse that pleased him, but the satisfaction. "I really put it to 'em," he laughed later.

At times of triumph, he laughed and smiled, but in days of defeat he seemed to be driven by devils. A perfectionist, he demanded more of those around him than they sometimes were willing to give. A moody man, Foyt always went his own way, concentrating almost completely on his career. A proud man, he sought triumphs others hadn't attained. After 1964, having won in Grand National racing once, he wanted to win there again and again.

In January of 1965, on the day after his 30th birthday, Foyt flew into Southern California to drive in the first NASCAR Grand National race of the new season, the Riverside 500. Late in the race, Dan Gurney, Junior Johnson and Marvin Panch were running one-two-three. As the big cars slowed going into the second corner of the twisting road course, Foyt closed in at 140 miles per hour.

As he tried to slow down to take the turn behind them,

his foot drove the brake pedal to the floorboard. His brakes had gone out! Foyt had a fraction of a second to decide on a course of action.

He later recalled, "You don't exactly reason it out. There's no time for debate. If you've been doin' this thing for a while, you get the picture right away and you react, almost by instinct.

"I didn't see how I could get by them on the high side. Maybe I could have missed Johnson, but not Panch. If I'd have hit him from behind, I'd have rode him up into the wall. I might've gotten away with it, but I don't think he could've. I didn't think I could cut underneath them and stay on the track, but that's what I figured I had to do. So, wham, away I went."

Foyt wrenched his steering wheel hard to the left, cutting down to the inside of the track. Desperately, he tried to straighten out, hanging on the rim of a sharp incline. Then he slid off and hurtled down a 15-foot embankment, bouncing end over end, as high as 40 feet at one point. The car landed in a steaming, crumpled heap on the infield grass. Fortunately, there was no fire.

A rescue crew rushed up, but Foyt was trapped in the tangle and it took 14 minutes to free him from the twisted metal. In agony, he was laid on a stretcher and rushed by ambulance to a nearby hospital. He had a fractured vertebra in his back and a broken left heel. His body was rubbed raw and badly bruised. "All the skin was scraped off my left ear and the left side of my face," he reported later. "My ears were slightly cauliflowered. My chin was badly bruised. My lips were swollen almost double. My feet, elbows and rear end were bruised so bad they turned black."

The force of the terrible tumble was so great that the

brand new coveralls he wore simply split apart and his crash helmet was dented in, but the heavy roll-bar protection built into the stock car saved his life.

At first he was listed in "fair condition" in the intensive care ward, but by the second day he was joking, "Now I've got to order me some new crash helmets."

His wife worried by his side, hoping he would retire, but he never considered it. Logically, it was time for him to quit, but Foyt was not a logical man. "Shoot, you can't let things like this get you down," he said.

He started to get around on crutches, but soon discarded them. By the time he was released from the hospital a month later, he had lost 25 pounds. But he began to build himself back up almost immediately by lifting weights and by swimming.

Near the end of March, less than three months after his smash-up, he flew to Arizona and limped into

Foyt recovers in a hospital after his spectacular crash at Riverside.

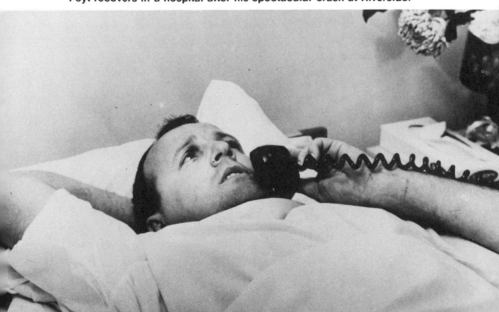

Phoenix Raceway to drive in a 100-mile event for championship cars. Friends and foes in the drivers' fraternity were surprised to see him and rushed over to welcome him and kid him. "I flew like a bird," A.J. chuckled.

Showing the stuff he was made of, he led all drivers in qualifying and led the race until his car sputtered to a stop. His cars broke, but Foyt didn't.

One week later, still strapped into a brace beneath his coveralls and unable to completely disguise his limp, the tough Texan traveled to Georgia to drive a new Ford in the Atlanta 500. Surprised, a writer asked why he was there.

"I'm a racing driver. Where else should I be?" he replied. Stuffing his hands into his leather jacket, he moved off to his car.

Freddie Lorenzen said, "He's hurting so bad he can't sleep nights, but you can't get the sonofabuck to admit it."

The race was run on a scorching day. A third of the way through it, Foyt came charging up on his old friend from the Riverside smash-up, Marvin Panch. (Today, Panch was Foyt's teammate, also driving a Ford.) As A.J. went to pass, the throttle on his car stuck. Heading into a turn, he was unable to slow down. The situation was similar to the one at Riverside, but this time Foyt spotted an opening on the outside.

"I thought, uh-oh, here we go, Riverside all over again," A.J. recalled later, "only this time I had a place to put her. I went flying high, wide and handsome."

Panch said, "I saw him go past me out of control, I felt it when he hit the wall and I just didn't want to think about what might have happened."

However, Foyt's car scraped to a safe stop and he walked away unhurt this time, cursing his bad luck.

He sat on a pit wall watching the race awhile, then began to pack up to fly to his next engagement in Phoenix. Panch was still leading the race, but the heat was getting to him. Suffering from heat exhaustion and neck cramps, he signaled that he needed a relief driver. The Wood brothers asked A.J. to take over. He jammed on his helmet and when Panch pulled in and got out, Foyt jumped in and took off.

There were 122 laps left of the 334-lap event and Foyt fought to hold the lead. Of 44 starters, only 14 finished the race but A.J. was one of them. Despite the brace on his back and the pain, A.J. battled Bobby Johns bitterly and flashed across the finish line in front. Throwing an arm around Panch, he recalled his close call in the race. "I was beginning to think I'd used up all my luck," he said with a smile. They divided the driver's share of the $18,000 first-place prize.

In 1966 A.J. won the Firecracker 400 again. But for the next few years, he was able to run only a few Grand National events and didn't win any. He won his third Indianapolis 500 and an unprecedented fifth USAC driving crown in 1967 and followed it by winning the 24 Hours of LeMans with Dan Gurney.

In the late 1960s and early '70s, however, his victories in USAC races became so infrequent that fans concluded he had passed his peak. It was on the Grand National tour for stock cars that aging A.J. proved he still could beat the best. In 1971 he was signed by the Wood brothers and put one of their Mercuries on the pole for the Daytona 500 at better than 182 miles per hour. He led the race until he ran out of fuel with 100 miles left.

After a push back to the pits for fuel, he got back to the track in eighth place, a lap behind the leader. He fought back to third place and was closing in on Richard Petty when the race ran out.

Next, he took the pole at above 151 miles per hour, led nine times and won the Miller 500 at Ontario, California, finishing eight seconds in front of Buddy Baker and 11 seconds in front of Petty.

In April he took the pole at above 155 mph, led most of the way and won the Atlanta 500, just two seconds ahead of Petty. Petty had taken the lead with 25 miles left, but Foyt stuck to his tail, caught him on the last turn of the last lap and outsprinted him to the checkered flag. By then Foyt was the star of the Wood brothers' team, the top driver of the best mechanical team on tour. A great driver like David Pearson was held in reserve, moved into the machine by the Woods only when A.J. was unavailable.

At Ontario in March 1972, Foyt relaxes during the time trials (left). Above, the Wood Brothers crew tends his car during a pit stop.

In 1972 Foyt cashed in on the biggest payoff in the South, putting a Daytona 500 triumph alongside his three Indianapolis 500 victories. Foyt forged his way through smash-ups and crippled cars to lead for the last 300 miles. At the finish he was a full lap ahead of runner-up Chargin' Charlie Glotzbach. His average speed of 161 miles per hour set a new Daytona 500 record, and he won $38,400.

Then he repeated his triumph in the Ontario 500, leading 145 of the 200 laps to finish four seconds in front of Petty. During the race, he dueled daringly with Petty, king of the southern stockers. Petty got so close behind Foyt at one point that he banged his car from behind. When Richard passed him, A.J. passed him back, squeezing through an inside opening so small that he scraped Petty's car as he barged by.

Later, weary and sweat-streaked in his soiled white coveralls, he stood in the press box. A writer suggested to A.J. that he had to work harder for this victory than he did for last year's.

Foyt said flatly, "They're all hard."

"Last year's was easy," the writer insisted.

Foyt fixed him with a chill look and snapped, "None of them are easy. They may look easy sitting up here, but they're not easy driving down there."

In 1973 Foyt began driving a Chevy in stock car competition, and it was not competitive. He had left the Wood brothers and he didn't win any of his three NASCAR races. He also failed to win in '74.

At 40 years old, Foyt seemed to be approaching the end of his career, although he was driven by a desire to win a fourth time at Indy. On the NASCAR circuit he had won seven important events on super-speedways and had earned around $300,000. Over all, he had won nearly $2 million in all kinds of racing.

Perhaps nothing dramatized Foyt's competitive skill more than his defeat in the Daytona 500 in 1974. A piece of Donnie Allison's exploding tire pushed Foyt's windshield out of its frame. Having started far back in 35th position, he completed his charge to fifth place at the finish, steering with one hand while holding the windshield in place with the other.

After Richard Petty won the race, he laughed and said, "Ol' A.J. always said he could beat us country boys with one hand behind his back and he dang near done it. He may not be a regular on our circuit, but any time he turns up I figure he's the one to beat. By now he's just about one of us, like family. Any place they're running cars, he's at home."

LEEROY
YARBROUGH

Florida Flash

When LeeRoy Yarbrough was barely in his teens, he started souping up old jalopies and testing their speed on a sandy strip of wasteland just outside his hometown of Jacksonville, Florida. Later he and his buddies would play "bumper tag" through the streets of the city.

"Man, when I think of the way we went when I didn't have any better sense, it scares me," he said years later.

Born in September of 1938, he grew up dreaming of driving in the biggest sporting event in his state—Daytona. His hero was another Floridian, Fireball Roberts. A poor boy, LeeRoy quit school in the tenth grade to go racing. Before he was 16, he lied about his age to get a driver's license and began to run an old jalopy on bush-league "outlaw" tracks.

Soon he went to work, driving a truck like his dad. On the side, he worked as a mechanic setting up race cars for better-known drivers. And he drove in every race he could make on the dirt ovals of Jacksonville. Within a few years LeeRoy was the man to beat. One season he was so successful that promoters put a bounty on his head. "Beat Yarbrough and win a $500 bonus," they told the other drivers.

LeeRoy first drove in a Grand National race in 1960 when he was 22. He began to drive NASCAR's sportsman car circuit in 1962 and won 37 races that year, including the Permatex 300, which is run annually at Daytona as a prelude to the 500 for big cars. That same year, he raced in about a dozen Grand National events, but on the big circuit he was a "no-name" who won no races and gained no attention.

A handsome, husky curly-haired fellow, he was already a cocky character. He was a loner who made few friends. He bragged about his ability to newsmen and ignored the fans. Few people around the profession liked him, and he had trouble getting good rides from the factory teams.

"In those early years on the Grand National circuit," he explained, "I owned the car I was driving or had built it for somebody else. Blood, sweat and tears usually were tied up in it. I had to do all the work, and I didn't have time to stop and talk to anyone. I didn't care for the social life, and I still don't.

"I have to do a lot of talking around reporters that I don't really want to do. I talk myself up. I know it makes me sound cocky, but if I don't have confidence in my own ability, who will? If I have confidence, my crew will have confidence. I had to do the talking because I never had anyone to do it for me. I didn't belong to a team with a manager and a public relations man. I was on my own."

Like his hero Fireball Roberts, LeeRoy told anyone who asked that he was among the best on the circuit. If no one asked, he didn't go out of his way to say anything. He went his own way and concentrated on his career to the extent of excluding the outside world from his life.

In 1964 in the Sportsman Annual at Daytona he crashed at 150 miles per hour while attempting to avoid a collision. He was knocked unconscious as his car burst into flames, but he was pulled out to safety. He suffered severe burns and broken bones in his foot but recovered rapidly. Within a month, he was racing again. Typically brash, he called that accident his "biggest thrill in racing."

That year, he won two minor events, but the next year he won none. After five seasons of occasional Grand

Young LeeRoy Yarbrough poses beside his car in 1965.

National starts, he had won only two races and had not earned more than $15,000 a season.

Getting to the top in auto racing is a long, hard pull. Other athletes sometimes become famous by the time they reach 21, but in auto racing it takes years to master all the tricks of the trade, build up confidence and gain the support of a top team. Few drivers become consistent winners before they are 30.

In 1966 LeeRoy Yarbrough won only one race in nine starts on the Grand National circuit, but his victory was a big one—the National 500 at Charlotte. At 28, he had finally won a super-speedway classic. Starting in 17th position, he roared into the lead on the 28th lap and never lost it. He finished five seconds ahead of Darel Dieringer. In 1967 Yarbrough won only one minor race in 15 starts. He had yet to earn as much as $25,000 in a season.

LeeRoy won only two races in 1968. But with 15 first-five finishes in 26 starts, he won more than $85,000 and began to be recognized as a promising driver. However, in the circuit's biggest event, the Daytona 500, he lost through a heartbreaking misunderstanding. He was leading late in the race when his crew flashed a sign reading "P1." It meant "place 1—you are ahead," but LeeRoy thought it meant "pit in one lap. After making a needless stop, he was caught by Cale Yarborough ten miles from the finish, and he lost to "the Yarborough with the extra *o*" by inches.

His one big win of the season was the Dixie 500 at Atlanta, but even that wasn't enough to make up for the year's frustrations. "Unlucky" LeeRoy complained, "I have won the pole position in races six times, been fastest qualifier eight times and led every race I have run, but have lost to bad luck or breakdowns. This can be a tough, frustrating profession. You and your crew can work your rear ends off around the clock, prepare a car perfectly and have a ten-cent part break and beat you. This is one sport in which man is at the mercy of a machine. No matter how good they're built, machines break down."

LeeRoy could only hope that the law of averages would catch up with him. "If you build them good enough and the man running them is good enough, you'll have your year sooner or later," he concluded hopefully.

His year was 1969. Few in car racing ever have had one like it. Yarbrough, who had won only six races on this circuit in his eight-year career, won a record seven super-speedway classics in this single season, finished in the first five in more than half his 30 starts and earned a record $188,000 in prizes.

It started in the Daytona 500, the race he had lost by a single second the year before to Cale Yarborough. Buddy Baker and Bobby Isaac drove Dodge Chargers onto the front row in qualifying time trials, but LeeRoy's Ford was ready on race day. Baker broke out on top, but Cale Yarborough caught him on the fourth time around and held the lead for almost 50 miles. Then Donnie Allison's Ford flew to the front. Pressing to recapture the lead, Cale crashed his car into a concrete retaining wall. He escaped with minor injuries, but he was out of the race.

Chargin' Charlie Glotzbach put his Dodge Charger in front near the halfway point. Allison's engine was souring. Meanwhile LeeRoy and A.J. Foyt, both driving Fords, had driven within range of the leaders. With 100 miles to go, Foyt and Allison fell back, leaving LeeRoy to challenge Glotzbach by himself. With 75 miles to go, LeeRoy leaped into the lead. But with 50 miles to go, Glotzbach got it back when LeeRoy had to pit to replace worn tires.

By the time LeeRoy returned he had fallen far back, but he battled back closer and closer to the leader. With 35 miles to go, Glotzbach made a fast pit stop, and his lead dwindled to eight seconds. Lap by lap, Yarbrough, a smooth, steady driver, cut down the distance between himself and the leader. It seemed certain he would have to settle for second place for the second season running, but he wouldn't give up.

With ten of the two-and-a-half-mile laps left, LeeRoy was within four seconds of the lead. With six laps left, he was within three seconds. With two laps left, he was within one second. As they entered the last lap and took the white flag, LeeRoy was within ten feet of Charlie. Glotzbach weaved wide and wild to cut off Yarbrough's passing lanes and prevent any drafting.

As they tore into the third turn, they came upon a slower car which had to be lapped. LeeRoy grabbed the low road, passing the other car on the inside. Charlie had to take the high road, swinging wide to get around the slower machine, which cost him time. LeeRoy had cleverly maneuvered into the lead.

Now, as they headed into the homestretch, it was Yarbrough weaving back and forth across the track to prevent a pass by Glotzbach. As they flashed toward the finish line with the fans screaming them on, Chargin' Charlie grabbed a momentary opening and drew almost abreast of LeeRoy. However, as they crossed under the checker, the nose of the Ford was in front.

In Victory Circle, the supposedly cold Yarbrough

wept. "Winning this one like this after losing the one last year the way I did, I just can't help it," LeeRoy gasped between gulps of oxygen. He was exhausted after a race in which speeds had at times exceeded 200 miles per hour. He was drenched with sweat and his hands were blistered. His average speed even with slowdowns was a record 157 mph. The tears touched a sensitive chord in the hearts of many. His human, emotional response that day won him a lot of friends.

Yarbrough was reaching for the heights. Four laps from the finish in the Rebel 400 at Darlington, LeeRoy had a dangerous moment. He was running just behind Bobby Allison and Cale Yarborough when Cale tried to pass Allison on the inside. Allison ran up high, brushed the rail, picking up a "Darlington stripe," slid sideways and sideswiped LeeRoy. The two spun as though one through the second turn. Allison crashed into a concrete barrier, but LeeRoy straightened out and tore past the surprised Cale to come in first.

Next, LeeRoy won the World 600 at Charlotte by two laps. But he lost the Atlanta 500 to Cale, then lost the Motor State 400 in Michigan when Cale rode him into the wall on the last lap.

In the Firecracker 400 at Daytona, LeeRoy barged by Buddy Baker with 50 miles to go and beat him home by 50 feet, averaging more than 160 miles per hour in a brilliant race. Before the Dixie 500 at Atlanta LeeRoy was so sick from a virus that he said publicly he doubted he could go the distance. But he grabbed the lead at the midway mark and moved on to win by a half-mile.

Then at Darlington in the Southern 500, he hit an oil slick, slid into a wall and mashed in the front end of his car. He returned to the pits, had the bent metal ripped off

In 1969 LeeRoy races his sleek Mercury at Riverside . . .

and got back on the track, racing hard. The event was interrupted by rain for four hours, then resumed.

As the day grew dark, it was clear the race would have to be curtailed short of the scheduled distance. As the cars neared 300 miles, LeeRoy caught and passed David Pearson, his Ford teammate. Pearson passed him back and swerved around to hold him off. But when they threw the white flag to tell the leaders they were on their last lap, LeeRoy darted around David and charged under the checkered flag to win when the race was called at 316 miles.

. . . and acquires a "Darlington stripe" in his Rebel 400 victory.

He wrapped up his super season with an unprecedented seventh super-speedway victory in the American 500 at Rockingham. He was the first driver ever to win at five super-speedways—Daytona, Darlington, Charlotte, Atlanta and Rockingham—in a single season. Few have turned this trick in an entire career. He brought glory to stock car racing by becoming the first NASCAR driver ever selected as "Driver of the Year" for the Martini and Rossi trophy in competition with Indianapolis championship car drivers and the glamour guys of the Grand Prix circuit.

Suddenly wealthy after a life of struggle and disappointment, the hard-luck king of the high banks had become the sport's newest superstar. Allowing himself a rare grin, LeeRoy said, "I guess it's a pretty good business after all."

Admitting that he could remember when he couldn't afford to buy a pair of shoes, Yarbrough said, "Goin' to work is fun now. All you got to do is go 200 miles per hour and beat off a bunch of 4,000-pound metal monsters for a few hours.

"I like everything about racing. I like the competition. I like the pay. I like the people in it. Dangerous? Certainly it is. But if driving a racing car worried me, I wouldn't drive one. Other people enjoy playing cards or going dancing; I enjoy racing at high speeds. I'm happy when I'm running fast. I'm relaxed. It's my fun as well as my business."

LeeRoy Yarbrough's brief run of good fortune began to run out in 1970. After winning seven super-speedway events in 1969, he helped win one and won just one on his own in 1970. After his car broke down in the World 600 at Charlotte, he drove relief for Donnie Allison in the late stages of the longest Grand National event. David Pearson led by two laps when LeeRoy leaped into the Allison auto, but when the clutch in Pearson's car caved in, LeeRoy went past him to win, sharing the prize money with Allison. Driving a Mercury for Junior Johnson, he stalked the leaders for 300 miles in the National 500 at Charlotte, took the lead in the late laps and won by a few feet from Bobby Allison when the event ended under the yellow caution signals with no passing permitted.

Otherwise, he had hard luck. He drove the Indianapo-

Grown older and huskier, LeeRoy chats with Richard Petty in 1972.

lis 500 for the third time without success. In 1967 he had spun out twice. In 1969 his open cockpit car had qualified eighth fastest but broke down early in the race. Now in 1970 his car caved in at the midway mark. Later in 1970 in another race for championship cars, the rich California 500 at Ontario, he was leading late in the race when his engine blew up in a flash of fire.

In 1971 luckless LeeRoy was stricken with Rocky Mountain fever, an unusual and severe illness. For a while he was not expected to survive. "They didn't exactly tell me I was going to die. They just told me to get all my personal things in order. When they tell you that, you don't sleep much at night," he admitted later.

After 40 days in the hospital, he had beaten the odds and was released, but he had still not recovered. He lost a lot of weight and his strength was sapped. Attempting a comeback, he suffered relapses. He returned to competition in 1972, but while he was third at Dover and fourth in a couple of big races, he couldn't win any. He had lost his edge. Disappointment diminished his desire. He retired in 1973 to leave the racing to others, at least for the time being—Petty, Pearson, the Allisons, the Yarborough with the "o," and all the rest.

CALE YARBOROUGH

Carolina Charger

There is no typical race driver. They are tall and short, fat and skinny, loud and quiet, aggressive and withdrawn. Some are smarter than others and some braver. But Cale Yarborough fit the public concept of what a race driver should be. He was short and husky, a natural all-around athlete and absolutely fearless. He did wild things off the track that made life on the track seem almost tame. But he seemed to have been born to race. Being a race driver was all he ever wanted to be.

He was born William Caleb Yarborough in March 1939 on a 500-acre tobacco farm in Timmonsville, South Carolina, and grew up harvesting crops and cutting timber. He would ride bulls in the barnyard and pull their tails to make them buck. He swam in a nearby river and sometimes dived head-first from an 80-foot-high cypress tree into water only five feet deep. He and his pals used to compete at catching snakes bare-handed. Poisonous ones counted double. He once wrestled an alligator at a carnival.

Years later, a friend who liked sky-diving asked Cale if he'd ever tried the sport. Cale admitted he hadn't. That day he made his first parachute jump, and later he made 20 more. One of these jumps almost ended in disaster. In a sky-diving exhibition at the Beaufort Water Festival in South Carolina, Cale missed the target area, which was a bay, and landed on the roof of a bank in a downtown shopping center. "A gust of wind got me and I still get kidded about missing the whole ocean," he said later with a smile.

He had always wanted to own a plane, so when he became successful as a driver, he and a friend bought one. They climbed in and Cale started it up and took off. After they'd been flying awhile, enjoying themselves, Cale suggested that the friend take a turn at the controls and land. The pal admitted he didn't know how to fly. Then Cale admitted he didn't know how, either. He'd just gotten in and learned on the job. So Cale landed the plane, not smoothly but safely. Later, he took pilot's lessons and flew his own twin-engined, six-passenger plane all across the country.

In high school Cale was an all-state fullback and had college offers, but he didn't like school. He did play semi-pro football for a few years. He became an amateur boxer and won most of his fights by knockouts, but did not turn pro. Ever since he was ten and his dad had taken him to see the Southern 500 at Darlington, 15 miles from the farm, Cale wanted to be a racing driver.

"I sat there all day with my fingers latched onto the wire fence, watching every move those men made," he

South Carolina's Cale Yarborough is all smiles in 1973.

recalled. "I thought race drivers were the greatest people in the world.

"I used to dream a lot. I would sit on a tractor plowing cotton and dream fantastic, impossible things—like piloting my own planes to races and getting my name in headlines for winning races—and I'd plow right into the next field."

Cale hitched rides to Darlington just to be around any races that were being run there. One official remembers chasing him out of the pits repeatedly when he was a teen-ager. He'd sneak in, be chased out and sneak back in again.

He began racing in the local soap box derby. Then he got a motorcycle, learned to do tricks on it and performed at some carnivals. Before he left high school, he helped friends rebuild a jalopy that he would drive to school, work on at lunchtime, then race nights and weekends on bush league "outlaw" tracks.

At 17, four years before he was eligible, he lied about his age and began running minor NASCAR events. He even drove in the 1957 Southern 500 at 18. He talked someone into giving him the ride in a terrible car. He sneaked into the pits and into the car and took off. An official who knew he was under-age recognized him and hauled him out of the car during a pit stop. Cale sneaked back in and took off again. But at the next pit stop he was hauled out again and chased out of the arena.

He was determined and just kept trying. He got into four races in five years on the Grand National circuit, while driving lesser races on other tours. He won $85 one year, $200 another. In 1963 he got into eight races in a terrible car and earned less than $3,000. Herman "The Turtle" Beam, a driver from Tennessee who got his nickname because he never went after a lead but ran slow and steady in an effort to finish races, turned over his car to Cale. Cale surprised everyone by putting it in front in a few events, but it always broke down before the finish. Cale and Beam were their own pit crew, and sometimes they even borrowed fuel from rival crews.

All this time Cale logged and farmed on the side to keep going. He had gotten married, and his wife Betty Jo was sympathetic to his desire to race. She encouraged him to keep trying. When he had saved a little money, he invested it in a turkey farm. "I lost my shirt, my money and the farm, too," he reported with a laugh. "I figured I better try a little harder to be a racer."

He went straight to racing director Jacque Passino of the top Ford team and asked for factory support in 1964. Passino was impressed by the stocky youngster's brashness and said, "I'll help you, but the first time you mess up, you're history."

In Yarborough's second race for Ford, he slid out of control trying to avoid an accident and flipped three times. When Cale called Passino and told him what had happened, Passino said calmly, "That wasn't your fault. No problem. We'll give you another car."

So Cale drove the new car until the Rebel 300 when he was sidelined with a burnt piston. He told Passino it had been all right the week before. Passino asked him if he had checked it before the race. Cale admitted he hadn't. Passino said, "You just messed up."

Cale went back to the bush tracks, then quit in disgust. He was working and playing semi-pro football when Passino called to offer him a job—as a handyman with the Holman-Moody team. Cale was back in racing, but after two full years on tour and 42 starts, he had finished

In the 1965 Daytona 500, Cale (21) races neck and neck with LeeRoy Yarbrough. Cale crossed the finish line inches ahead of LeeRoy.

in the first five only five times and still had not won a race.

In 1965 he got another chance as a driver with the former racer Banjo Matthews and his Ford team. Cale won only one minor race in 46 starts, but he did finish second in two super-speedway events. "The Carolina Charger" was beginning to show his stuff, but luck didn't seem to favor him. In a race at Darlington he lost control and flew over a fence. Aides rushed to the spot and found him sitting on the ground beside the car, kicking at the ground and cursing.

The next year, Ford sat out part of the season, sidelining most of its drivers, including Cale. The company returned to racing late in the season, but Cale was blanked in 14 outings. After ten years of trying, he had only one minor victory.

In 1967, however, Cale signed on with the Wood brothers' team. And that year he came through. Charging a hot car, he broke into the top ranks. He won only two of 14 starts, but they were big ones. The first was the Atlanta 500. After narrowly missing a collision with a car driven by Curtis Turner in the time trials, Cale led all but 32 of the 334 laps in the race itself.

His second big win was the Firecracker 400 at Daytona. Cale dueled dramatically over the final 55 miles with Dick Hutcherson and Darel Dieringer and came from third place on the last turn of the last lap, sling-shotting around both rivals to beat Hutcherson by less than one car length and Dieringer by two in an enormously exciting finish.

His big year was 1968. He won four super-speedway classics—and $136,000—in 21 starts.

At Daytona, he captured the pole with a record run, qualifying at just under 190 miles per hour, then ran the race at around 185 mph. He caught LeeRoy Yarbrough ten miles from the finish and whipped him at the wire to win by inches.

Later in the year he returned to Daytona to win the Firecracker 400 by a full lap with an average speed of 167 miles per hour, the fastest race ever. He won the Atlanta 500 for the second straight time, too, tying the single-season record of three super-speedway victories shared by Petty, Pearson and Lorenzen.

This brought Cale to his "dream race," the Southern 500 at Darlington, where he'd driven his soap-box racer down the main street as a boy. He was hot, but so were Petty, Bobby and Donnie Allison, Davey Pearson and LeeRoy Yarbrough.

Cale's car encountered problems early in the race.

Before he could clear them up, he had fallen two laps back. Once he got the car going right, however, it was faster than anything on the track, and he started the long run through traffic to unlap himself and get back into contention in the 364-lap event.

LeeRoy picked his way through a series of spectacular accidents to build a substantial early lead. But at 150 miles, Donnie Allison forged to the front. At 200 miles, Pearson pushed in front. At 300 miles, Cale began to challenge, and at 400 miles, he careened past Davey Pearson into the lead.

Through the final 100 miles, the two fought ferociously around the cramped oval. On the last lap, Pearson pulled even. As they came off the fourth turn, they were neck and neck as the spectators cheered themselves hoarse.

Through the homestretch, both drivers had their cars flat out. Cale had Davey by inches, and he would not give them up. As they flashed across the finish line, Cale still held onto that slim lead. After 500 miles of furious driving through tight traffic Cale had an unprecedented fourth super-speedway win in one season—by inches. The $47,250 he collected at Daytona was the biggest purse of his career.

In 1969 Cale topped Davey Pearson by three seconds to take the Atlanta 500 for the third year in a row. He also won the Motor State 400 in Michigan after a bitter battle with LeeRoy Yarbrough in which Cale drove LeeRoy right up into the wall on the first turn of the last lap.

Outsiders assumed Cale and LeeRoy were brothers, but they did not even spell their last names the same way and were bitter rivals rather than relatives. Cale lost the Rebel 400 at Darlington when he crashed into Bobby

Allison's car late in the race and LeeRoy rode by to win.

In December of 1969, Cale blew a tire and crashed into a concrete barrier at top speed in the first Texas 500. He suffered a smashed shoulder blade, breaking and splintering other bones in three places. He was unconscious seven days before he began to recover. One doctor observed that he had never before seen anyone survive such a bone-shattering crash. Predictions were that Yarborough would be sidelined at least six months, if not a full year.

However, just two months later, in February of 1970, the tough, durable driver was back in action in the Daytona 500. In March he was second in the Atlanta 500, and in May he was second in Charlotte's World 600. In June he won the Motor State 400 in Michigan, outlasting Daytona 500 victor Pete Hamilton in a Petty Plymouth by one-tenth of a second in a thrilling side-by-side finish. Then he topped Davey Pearson by two seconds on the American 500 in North Carolina.

His comeback complete, he admitted, "I was worried about being as good as ever, but I've always felt you can accomplish what you believe you can, and I believe in myself."

He confessed that while he loved racing, he found it rugged: "You're driving at an average 200 miles per hour, bumper to bumper, around and around in a tight circle. The temperature inside the car is 150 degrees, and you've been driving almost four hours. Every muscle in your body screams with pain, but you push and push, fighting that animal of a machine. Your mouth is full of dust and your head is full of noise.

"In most other sports, you can call time out, but there's no rest in a race. Let your mind stray for just one second and you're dead. They'll hose you out of the wreck, sweep you off the track and write your name on bronze someplace. You are strung out on tension, continually controlling your fear, turning it into what some might call courage.

"On one front, you're fighting the track, watching every ripple, every angle. On another you're listening to the scream of your engine, hearing noises that aren't there. During a race, it's like I become a machine and the machine becomes a man. I talk to my cars, baby them, shout at them, praise them. I feel them live and breathe in my hands.

"All this while in a psychological race with the man in front of you, the one alongside you, the one behind you. What will the one in front do when you try to pass him? What will you do when the next car tries to pass you? You wonder what he's thinking, while he wonders what you're thinking. You wonder what he'll do and what his car can do. You wonder if he's feeling the weariness, the pain, the muscle cramps you're feeling."

Twice, Cale cooperated with doctors trying to measure the strain that is exerted on race drivers in competition. They monitored his heart and pulse during two Southern 500s and discovered that these rates sometimes tripled under that sort of stress. Cale admitted he sometimes woke up in a cold sweat the night before a race, but said he was able to banish fear from his mind during a race so he could concentrate on driving.

Those close to him said he could relax after a victory, but brooded over defeats for days. He, himself, said, "You concentrate so intensely on a race that you are bound to carry it around with you for a while afterward. Your senses are so heightened in a race that in a car reeking of oil and fuel and sweat, wearing a mask and going close to 200 miles per hour, I have caught the scent of a tree blossoming 100 yards away. But I go to bed after a race with the sound of that big engine still ringing in my ears." Still, he insisted, "Winning money in races is different from working for it. It's like getting cash for having fun, I love it so much."

In 1971 Ford pulled out of racing again, and Cale wasn't sure whether the Wood brothers would compete either. He had driven a championship car at Indianapolis in 1966 and '67, failing to finish both times. But when he got an offer to switch to USAC and drive the championship trail, Cale agreed, attracted by the big money.

Cale discusses a race with Glen Wood of the Wood Brothers in 1968.

It didn't work. There are not many competitive cars on the USAC circuit, and Cale didn't have one of them. While Al and Bobby Unser, Mark Donohue, Mario Andretti, Joe Leonard, A.J. Foyt and others were running up front, Yarborough was struggling at the rear. At Indianapolis, his car broke down just short of 400 miles in 1971. In '72 he was still running at the finish, but was well back in tenth place. He didn't come close to winning a race on that tour.

Discouraged, he returned to NASCAR competition during 1972 with a renewed desire to win. Joining the Junior Johnson team in a Chevrolet prepared by Herb Nab, Yarborough failed to win a race and finished as high as fifth only once. But he bounced back in 1973 to win four races, finish in the first five 16 times and earn a career high of $162,000.

"It took us a year to get together and it took me a year to sort the car out," he reported.

After he topped Davey Pearson by a half-mile to win his second Southern 500, he said, "I've heard some mumblings about me being washed up, but I didn't pay any attention. I've been in position to win several races, but we simply had bad luck. It was downright discouraging, but we didn't get discouraged."

He went on to win the National 500 at Charlotte, outrunning Richard Petty. He also won the Nashville 250-miler and the Southeastern 500-lapper in Bristol, Tennessee. He led all 500 laps at Bristol in a blistering display of driving. By year's end, he had boosted his career record to 18 victories, a dozen of them in classics on super-speedways, and hoisted his earnings above the $600,000 mark.

In the Winston-Western 500 on Riverside's road

course in California in 1974, he tried to pass pole-sitter Pearson on the opening lap and raced side-by-side with him through three turns. On the fourth turn he lost control and spun across the course, narrowly missing the rest of the tightly bunched cars. When he rejoined the race he was in 35th and last position. But he drove daringly to work his way back into the lead just before the race was red-flagged for rain after 63 of the 191 scheduled laps.

The race was resumed a week later and Cale was leading by ten seconds with two laps left when he started to run low on fuel. To pit at that point would be to lose, so he took a chance, slowing down to save fuel, but not by so much that Richard Petty could catch him. Cale's gas tank ran dry as he crossed the finish, but he was three seconds in front.

Grinning in Victory Circle, he said, "I could see Richard in my rear-view mirror, but I didn't know whether to worry about him catching me or about me running out of fuel. I had just enough left to hold him off."

Later in the year, Cale won at Dover Downs and again at Riverside in the Tuborg 400. And he won the Atlanta 500 for the fifth time.

In 1974 he returned to Riverside at the start of the season to take the Winston Western 500. Rain halted the race after 140 miles, but when it was resumed the following weekend, Cale drove Junior Johnson's Chevy past the early leaders and beat Richard Petty by three seconds. In the Southern 500, Yarborough was the only survivor among the top contenders after a series of spectacular crashes. Only twelve of 40 starters completed the race, and Cale came home first.

Grimy and tired, Cale celebrates his victory in the 1973 National 500.

Other drivers won more super-speedway races in 1974, but Cale had a super season. He won several traditional classics on the short-track circuit. For example, he gained victory at the grueling Volunteer 500 in Bristol, Tennessee, by blasting past Buddy Baker on the final turn of the final lap. And at Martinsville in the Virginia 500, he led all but 23 of the furious 450 laps, finishing two seconds ahead of Richard Petty.

With such victories, Cale won more than $200,000 for the first time in his career. He had reestablished himself as a star on the NASCAR circuit. Stock car fans were happy to see the Carolina Charger back home. And Cale seemed happy to be there.

BOBBY ALLISON

Big Brother

This was the midsummer of 1966. On the NASCAR Grand National circuit, the drivers were on a northern swing. One of the drivers was Bobby Allison, a man of 28 in his third year on the tour. He had yet to win a race. Allison was running a beat-up Chevrolet Chevelle as an independent—without major commercial support. He had won only six or seven thousand dollars in three seasons, far less than he spent. He had used up most of the money he had saved or borrowed, and was nearly broke.

In a race at Binghamton, New York, Bobby's engine blew out, coming so completely apart it could not be rebuilt. For a factory team this would be a minor setback. For Allison it was a disaster. He was towing his car to Oxford, Maine, for the next race, trying to decide if he should sink his last few dollars into a new engine.

"I was close to quitting. I couldn't go on much further," he admitted. But he passed a Chevy dealer on his drive east and on an impulse he stopped and spent most of his remaining money for a new passenger car engine. He could not afford a high-powered racing engine. And when he got to the track in Oxford, he went to a garage down the street and went to work on the new engine with the help of some friends who were serving as his pit crew.

They worked all through the night and right up until qualifying time. Bobby had only a few laps of practice before he went into his time trials, but to his surprise the engine performed almost perfectly, and he qualified for the pole position.

The track was a paved oval, one-third of a mile around. The race was a 100-miler, which meant 300 laps of almost continuous turning. In some ways such races are tougher than long ones on super-speedways. At least on a track a mile or more around, a driver could relax for a few seconds on the long straightaways.

David Pearson and Richard Petty were favored to win the Oxford race in their factory cars. Petty had car trouble, and Pearson took the early lead. Then Bobby Allison took over. "David and I had a pretty neat fender-to-fender duel through the first part of the race before I managed to pull away," he said. Then Jim Paschal made a run at Allison. "He was running pretty fast, but I was faster on that day," Bobby recalled.

It was one of those days when everything worked right. "I went the whole distance without refueling," Bobby said, " 'cause that little Chevy engine didn't gobble up the gasoline like some of the bigger power plants we have today. Even so, the chief steward thought for sure I'd have to pit for fuel. Near the end of the race, when there was a yellow flag, he stepped onto the track and hollered, 'Stop for gas!' I heard him, but I wasn't about to stop."

He went on to win. It was not only his first Grand National victory, but the first Grand National win for an independent in several seasons and the first win for a Chevy in three seasons.

"It was just a little ol' race that didn't pay much and didn't mean much, at least not to most, but it meant a lot to me and not only in money," Bobby recalled. "It kept me going. It is more memorable to me than any of the much bigger victories I've scored since. It's the one race above all others I've run that I'll never forget because it was the big one in making my career a success."

Factory teams had been pouring so much money, manpower and equipment onto NASCAR tracks that the independent operator no longer could compete successfully. Allison's was one of the last of the successful shoestring operations. That year and for four years after that he frustrated and embarrassed the factory Fords and Chryslers often enough to get the title "Mr. Independent."

Allison couldn't win consistently, but he could consistently challenge the winners, and he did average about five wins a season for five years. He was making a good living racing independently, but he finally went over to the big teams in 1971, seeking to compete successfully for the large prizes offered in the super-speedway races.

Robert Arthur (Bobby) Allison was born in December 1937, in Hueytown, Alabama, a tiny community of fewer than 6,000 people. A brother, Donnie, was born in

In 1967, a year after his first big breakthrough, Bobby Allison works on his car before the Southern 500 at Darlington.

September 1939, and became Bobby's buddy and competitor in a bid for car racing success.

"It was about all we ever wanted to do. Bobby got bit by the bug first, and I jus' naturally caught it from him," Donnie recalled. Bobby, the taller and older brother, got a headstart on Donnie and stayed ahead throughout most of their careers.

Although Bobby was born in and returned to settle in Hueytown, he grew up in Florida and attended high school in Miami, where he played some basketball and football, but lacked size or exceptional skill. He started racing at 17 in 1955 in a jalopy event. He slowly worked his way up, and by the early 1960s, he was driving modified stockers on NASCAR's smaller circuit for these cars. In 1962 and 1963 he won the driving title in the modified stocker classification.

"We bought a Chevelle out of a junkyard for $300 and rebuilt it in my backyard when we went into Grand National racing," Bobby remembered. "In all, we had about $5,500 invested in the car when we took it racing. As you travel there are a lot of expenses. And any accidents you have cost you a lot. It's a hard way to go, and we went hungry a few times along the way."

The big breakthrough was the 1966 victory in Maine. A few days later, on the track at Fonda, New York, Bobby's car slid into a chain-reaction pile-up and got smashed from behind. Bobby was able to walk away from the wreck, but his car required more costly repairs.

That was on a Thursday night. For 48 hours, Bobby, his friends, and some friendly rivals, including a driver named James Hylton, worked to put the car in running order again. On Saturday night in Islip, Long Island, in a 300-lapper on the tiny fifth-of-a-mile asphalt oval, Hylton was leading when he ran out of fuel nine laps from the finish. Ironically, Allison sped past to win.

Later in the season, Bobby's car exploded in flames during a pit stop, burning him and four others, one severely. Bobby suffered some second- and third-degree burns, but the accident did not scare him off. He won three races in 1966 and more than $20,000 in prizes, which gave the independent driver-mechanic the chance for a real run at the top teams.

In 1967 Allison drove Freddie Lorenzen's Ford Fairlane much of the time and scored six victories, including an eye-opening super-speedway triumph in the American 500 at Rockingham. He won by a full lap over Davey Pearson. In the last race of the season, the Western North Carolina 500 at Weaverville, Bobby won a lead-swapping, side-denting dash to the wire with Richard Petty by less than a car length.

Allison was the scourge of the small tracks. Operating primarily as an independent, driving his own Chevy, Bobby won two races and $50,000 in 1968 and five races and $65,000 in 1969. But he was disappointed by his inability to keep up with the factory teams on the big tracks. He had run strongly in some of the super-speedway events, but his cars were not consistent enough to win.

In 1970 Bobby lost the National 500 at Charlotte by a few feet. He might have won, but the closing laps were run under the yellow slowdown signals, so Allison was prohibited from passing leader LeeRoy Yarbrough. Bobby did bring home the bacon in a Dodge in the Atlanta 500, conquering Cale Yarborough in a sizzling stretch run, but it was one of only three races he won all season.

Allison flashes a big smile after winning the 1970 Atlanta 500.

Allison was so smooth and so consistent a driver that he finished second to Petty for the driving championship and earned more than $130,000 in prizes. But he was working hard for his money, starting about 40 races a season. And he had still not established himself as a superstar in his sport.

His opportunity came early in the 1971 season. He was offered the ride in the Holman-Moody Ford when the team lost its top driver, David Pearson, after a disagreement. Allison made the most of his chance. He won the World 600 at Charlotte, the Mason-Dixon 500 at Dover, the Motor State 400 in Michigan and the Golden State 400 at Riverside—all in the month of June!

Bobby was hot. Later in the season he lost by a car length to Petty in the Dixie 500 at Atlanta. Then he beat Petty by less than a car length to win the Yankee 400 in Michigan. And in the Talladega 500 he was involved in a savage three-car fight to the finish with Petty and Pete Hamilton. On the last lap, Allison sideswiped Petty, forcing him into Hamilton's car. As the three cars careened to the finish line, Allison was in front. The incident touched off a feud between Bobby and Petty which would not be settled for years.

In the Southern 500 at Darlington on Labor Day, Allison outran Petty from start to finish. In the National 500 at Charlotte (cut to 357 miles by a rainstorm), Bobby won his eighth super-speedway classic of the year, surpassing LeeRoy Yarbrough's record of seven. He won two lesser races on the tour, for a total of ten wins, and finished in the first five in 25 of 40 outings. He stood second to Richard Petty in the driver standings, and he earned $236,000, second only to Petty's earnings of $309,000. It was one of the greatest seasons any driver had ever enjoyed. Suddenly Bobby was one of the princes of car racing.

Holman and Moody broke up over the winter, but by then Bobby was in demand and had his choice of offers. He wanted to get back in a Chevy and joined the Junior Johnson team for 1972. Few thought he could match his 1971 performance, but he even surpassed it in some ways.

He won ten races for the second straight season. He again finished in the first five 25 times—in only 31 starts. Again he was second in the driver standings. And he increased his earnings to $271,000 for one year.

He won "only" six super-speedway races, compared to his eight in 1971. In the Atlanta 500 he flew from far back to top A.J. Foyt by a few inches at the flag. He came from behind on the last turn of the last lap and outraced Davey Pearson by three lengths to win a thrilling Southern 500. In the World 600, Buddy Baker led in the closing laps, but Bobby tapped Buddy's left rear fender to send him out of control for a few seconds, then blasted by him on the inside. Buddy pressed Bobby through the last three laps, but could not get by.

Allison could be a violent, vicious competitor. He had a series of savage skirmishes with Petty during the year. Allison claimed the fender-banging began in 1968 at Islip, Long Island. "Richard had the field lapped and looked like an easy winner," he said, "but when he came up behind me he began banging the rear of my car. He was trying to get me to move over to let him by, but I sure wasn't going to get off the track just to let Petty get past. He was the champion and I was no one at the time and I guess he thought I'd let him through. But I wouldn't and he bent his fender into his own tire and had to stop. I went on to win.

"Afterward, Richard's brother Maurice came up and said he wanted to talk to me. We went over by some parked cars and suddenly he decked me with a punch to the jaw. I wrestled him down and we went at it until others broke it up. The Allisons and Pettys have been going at it pretty good ever since."

Their worst rumble took place in the Wilkes 400 at North Wilkesboro, North Carolina, late in the 1972 season. They had been banging into one another in race after race, and this time Petty blocked Bobby from making a pass on the next-to-last lap. Allison forced his way alongside Petty on the inside, then drifted wide and forced his rival into the wall. Allison took the lead, but Petty chased him and caught him on the last lap. Petty banged into the rear of Allison's car, then darted past to win.

Petty admitted later, "This is getting danged dangerous."

Allison sighed and said, "It's the sort of a sport where you just can't let another driver run you off the track if you want to be around to win. I don't like it and I doubt that he likes it, but it's something sore between us which we can't seem to heal. We both love racing. No one wants to hurt anyone else to win. But everyone wants to win. It's a tough sport. And you have to drive tough."

Allison won the Martini and Rossi Trophy as "Driver of the Year" in '72. He was the third NASCAR driver in four seasons to win it, following LeeRoy Yarbrough in 1969 and Petty in 1971.

A devoted family man, an ardent fisherman and hunter, and a steady church-goer, Allison was also active in civic affairs around his Alabama hometown. He became a spokesman for his sport, and many believed he

Bobby (12) screeches around a turn on the road course at Riverside just ahead of his arch-rival, Richard Petty, in 1973.

was the most admired man in stock car racing. His public appeal was demonstrated when the fans voted him the most popular driver three straight seasons. It also was noteworthy that in 1973 his rival drivers voted him the most popular driver in the fraternity.

Yet on the track, Bobby Allison was always a driver who would not give a break to a competitor nor ask one in return. "I consider myself a competitor, but I fight fair," he said. "I won't hit a man first, but if he hits me first, I'll hit him back. I won't give ground to any man."

Not even to his own brother. Bobby battled Donnie as bitterly as any other rival. "If I can't win, I'd want Donnie to win," he said, "but I want to win. On the track he's just another driver in another car who I want to beat real bad. We're close. We feel for one another. But we also do our best to beat one another."

Going back on his own, operating independently, Bobby had a difficult season in 1973. He won only two races, but he still took home over $100,000. By year's end he had won 41 Grand National races, which made him one of the top ten all-time winners. And he had won 17 super-speedway classics, which trailed only David Pearson's 23 and Richard Petty's 22. Then in 1974, after more than ten years on tour, Bobby became the third stock car driver in history to win a million dollars in his career, following Petty and Pearson into that exclusive circle.

The sport's showcase event, the Daytona 500, was the only prestige event on this circuit which escaped Bobby Allison. "I want to win it, but I can't say going for it is the only thing which keeps me going," Bobby said.

"Some say it's time for me to retire. This good ol' boy is getting old. But it was a long, rough ride to the top and I like it here. Davey Pearson had a long, rough ride to the top, too. Like me, he had a lot of lean years. A lot of guys have gotten fat in recent years. The tour's twice what it used to be. A man hesitates steppin' off to the side of this here road these days."

DAVID PEARSON

Li'l David

Richard Petty may be the greatest stock car race driver of all time, but he once called David Pearson "the best driver NASCAR's got." Glen Wood, who had had such stars as Curtis Turner, Freddie Lorenzen, A.J. Foyt and Cale Yarborough driving for him, also favored Pearson. "I tell David all the time he's the best I ever had," he said. Judgments on who is *the* best stock car driver may differ, but it is clear that David Pearson was one of the top four or five.

Pearson was a shy and modest man, a withdrawn, soft-spoken sort. He never became a public spokesman for his sport because he lacked the polish and confidence. "I jus' don't have the education to speak at banquets and such, and it depresses me because I love racing," he confessed.

He got the nickname "Li'l David" not because he was

small but because he defeated many stock car giants, just as the biblical David defeated Goliath. In 1961 he was in his second year on the tour, when he suddenly hit the headlines with three surprising super-speedway wins. He upset all the favorites, and a big future seemed to be ahead of him. But he was not ready to follow up such success, and for the next few years he was considered a disappointment, struggling along a rough road back to the top.

"A lot of people gave up on me," he said, looking back, "but I never gave up on myself. I wanted it too much. I had ability, but I needed experience. I got lucky early, but I had a lot to learn."

His handsome face showed traces of his Cherokee

Li'l David Pearson straps on his helmet and gets set to race.

Indian ancestry, but Pearson was a typical southern
small-town boy. He was born in 1934 and raised in the
tiny mill town of Whitney, near Spartanburg, in South
Carolina. His father and mother worked hard in the
cotton mills to earn a living for their family, and David
developed powerful arms and shoulders lifting heavy
spools of cotton to help out. He quit school at 16.

"From the time I was ten and saw my first race, from
the time I was a little shaver, racing was all I ever
wanted," he once said. "Me and my buddies used to
sneak over the old board fences at the Spartanburg
Fairgrounds and watch the stock cars flying on that dirt
track, and I always knew that was for me."

His older brother owned a body repair shop, and
David volunteered to sweep the place just so he could be
near the beat-up racers that were brought in. On the
country roads around Whitney, he would race anyone
who'd challenge him or take up his challenge, even if his
wife-to-be was in the car. Helen Pearson remembered,
"David sure got in a lot of races on the streets and never
lost a one that I can recall. It always scared me to death,
and I'd yell for David to stop and let me out. He'd laugh
at that."

In 1952, when David was 18, he married Helen. Four
months after their first child was born, Pearson bought
an old racing car for $40 and told his wife he was going
racing. Helen offered to go to work to support him if he'd
agree not to race, but he wouldn't. "He told me I'd just
have to get used to him being a race driver," Helen said.
"So I did."

David fixed up his car and entered it in a race at
Woodruff Speedway in September 1953, finishing second
and winning $13. His mother was also worried and

offered him $30 if he'd sell his car. He took her money and sold the car for $70. With his profits, he bought another car. She, too, could see it was hopeless.

"I was hooked on it and nothing and no one was going to stop me," he said.

Pearson had the enthusiasm, but in the beginning he didn't have the know-how. "I didn't know anything about how to set up a car for races," he recalled. "Some of my buddies were helping me and they knew about what I knew. We thought the car had to lean to the left like all good race cars, so we all jumped up and down on the left running board of my old jalopy and actually knocked it over to one side. We used iron from an old bed for roll bars. That's what we knew."

But he learned. Driving on local dirt tracks week after week, he soon began to get a reputation as a winner. Describing his early years in racing, he said, "You eat dirt and push old worn-out cars on dimly lit tracks and hope you get a break before you get killed. The old tracks tear up the cars, and it keeps you working just to keep going. If you're a winner, it's even tougher. You're like the gunman in a western movie. You have the reputation, and everyone is after you to see if you're really good. Some of the small tracks even put a bounty on your head—a bonus to the driver who knocks off the top man."

By 1959 he had joined NASCAR's sportsman circuit, and that year he won 30 of 42 races and the South Carolina state championship. "I could have won more, but I had to lose a few on purpose or I'd lose a place to race," he admitted. "If one driver always won, fan interest fell off. The promoters told me if I won five races in a row, they'd kick me out. So I'd win four and lead the

fifth until the last lap when I'd pull over and let somebody else win."

He didn't like that much, and determined to move up to the big time, but he didn't have the money. "I was working in a service station days and racing nights," he recalled, "but I was doing so good on the dirt tracks some of my friends wanted to see how I could do on the super-speedways. The owner of the service station, a local cop and my father started a drive to raise money to send me on the circuit. My policeman friend even went

In the 1962 World 600, David Pearson (3) is on the front line with old-timer Fireball Roberts as the cars complete their pace lap. Pearson scored a big upset victory in his Ray Fox Pontiac.

on the radio station in town to appeal to the public for funds to buy me a car. So I got me a car."

It wasn't enough of a car. He didn't win any races during 1960, but he came close several times and did well enough in 22 starts to be named "Rookie of the Year" on the Grand National tour.

That showing earned David his big chance—a factory

ride with the Pontiac team operated by Ray Fox. David grabbed it and shocked the circuit in his sophomore season by winning three super-speedway classics—the World 600 at Charlotte, the Dixie 400 at Atlanta and the Firecracker 250 at Daytona.

His wife remembered that first triumph at Charlotte vividly. "I watched the race from the infield," she recalled, "and I wasn't scared until a driver had a real bad crack-up. Later, he lost his leg. I shuddered at David having to continue the race after such a horrible accident, but he was leading and he did go on to win.

"Everyone came running up to me and started yelling about how much David had won. I couldn't even see them because tears were rolling down my face. An official came to take me to the winner's circle. When I got there David was kissing some gal movie star."

She laughed wistfully. "That first race, David earned $28,000 and a new convertible. His cut was $12,000, including the car, the first new one we'd ever owned. When he told me he wanted to put the money into a house, I was thrilled. We decided our home would be in the same mill village surroundings that we both knew and loved. I was really proud of David when he told me he didn't care for a big house with a lot of fancy trimming. Maybe he knew it wouldn't always be as easy as it was that year."

Pearson earned almost $50,000 in purses that year. "I don't know how I did it," he said years later. "I wasn't that good, only I didn't know it. I'm a charger, I had a good car, it held up and I won. I soon found out I had a lot to learn, however. I had to learn how to win in a car that wasn't way out the best. I learned how to win by losing a lot."

During the next six years he didn't win a single super-speedway event. In fact, in 1962 and 1963 he did not win a race of any sort. After 1962, Ray Fox let him go and Pearson drove Dodges for Cotton Owens, a championship driver who had retired. He drove them so hard they kept breaking on him.

"He was still wild," Owens recalled. "At Richmond in 1964 I told him I could still beat him even though I was washed up, because I had more experience even if he had more talent. I had two equal cars and I gave him his choice. He took one, I took the other one and I won. After that, he was more likely to listen to my advice."

Pearson won eight races in 1964. The next year he won only two, but he finished in the top ten in more than half his starts. He was improving, and in 1966 he won 15 races, the driving championship and almost $50,000. He began to enjoy life again.

But Pearson was still not winning on the super-speedways. Owens' sponsors were pressuring him to produce some big wins, and the two started to blame each other for their failures. In 1967 they parted ways and Pearson joined Dick Hutcherson's team. He started only 22 races and won only two. Race fans began to suspect that he really wasn't a top driver after all, but David refused to get discouraged.

"It's a funny game," he said. "Stock car racing is two ends of the world. You win and you're at the very top. You're surrounded by fans. You're a great driver and a great guy. You blow a tire, blow an engine, strip a gear, hit a wall or do any one of the thousands of things that can keep you from Victory Lane and you're a nobody.

"It's like a giant carnival, on the move from town to town. Every track is different, and you have to set up to meet a new challenge every week. There are nights of sleeping in the truck, of working until daylight in the garage just to pick up a $15 tow fee to get you to the next race. It takes most of what you win, even when you win consistently, to keep on the road from race to race and to keep your car in condition to run again and again. Without solid sponsorship support you can't win. There's a lot of work and heartache from the bottom to the top."

When Freddie Lorenzen suddenly retired in 1967, Holman and Moody were looking for a top driver for their Ford, and they took a chance on Pearson. Moving into a car which could run the long tracks as well as the short, Pearson proved himself once and for all. He won 16 races in 1968, finished among the first five in 36 of 48 events, won his second driving title and earned almost $120,000, the third highest one-season haul in history.

He also ended his long drought on the super-speedways. He leaped into the lead on lap 240 of the treacherous track at Darlington and pulled away in the final 50 laps to win the Rebel 400, almost a lap ahead of Darel Dieringer and Richard Petty. He wept in the pits. "You wait and wait and lose close and lose close and suddenly you win big. It's hard to figure," he said.

Pearson scored another noteworthy victory that year at Bristol, a town that straddles the state line between Tennessee and Virginia. The Southeastern 500 is a 500-lap, 250-mile race. It is an exhausting event on a high-banked, half-mile paved oval.

From the first, Pearson and Richard Petty flew ahead of the pack. At 100 laps, LeeRoy Yarbrough and Cale Yarborough drove past them and into the lead. At 200 laps, Petty pressed to the front. At 300 laps, Pearson led again. The front-runners swapped the lead back and forth in a series of dazzling maneuvers on the short, dangerous track. At 400 laps, Petty was ahead again.

Yarbrough shot in front, Pearson passed him and then Petty passed both of them. The excitement was enormous. With 20 laps left, Pearson held the edge. With ten laps left, Petty was in front. With five laps left, Pearson pulled even with Petty but couldn't pass him. With four laps left, he got by. With three laps left, Petty put his Plymouth in front again. With two laps left, Pearson gained the lead again. They raced through the last lap and down the homestretch side by side. At the finish line, Pearson's Ford was in front by an inch or two. After hours of pounding speed on a scorching hot day, a few inches made the difference.

The next season, 1969, was a banner year for Pearson. He broke the 190-mile-per-hour barrier at Daytona, although he didn't win the big race. He did win the Yankee 400 in Michigan, the Carolina 500 and nine other races. He also finished in the first five a remarkable 42 times in 51 starts to become the first driver ever to win two straight driving titles.

But once again he was due for disappointments. In 1970 he won the Rebel 400 at Darlington by three laps, but it was his only victory all year. He was leading the World 600 at Charlotte with two laps to go when his clutch gave way and his car coasted to a stop. He earned more than $85,000, but the money did not make up for his frustrations.

It would get worse before it would get better. When Ford withdrew its factory support of stock car racing, Holman and Moody tried to cut back. Pearson refused to take a cut in pay, however, and he resigned from the team. Once again there was talk that David was finished.

In 1971 he got into only 17 races and won only two minor ones.

He started the 1972 season without a regular ride, then accepted an offer to back up A.J. Foyt on the Wood brothers' team, driving whichever NASCAR races Foyt couldn't attend. It was a demeaning situation for a driver with David's credentials, but he put his pride aside. "Sometimes getting kicked around gives a guy a lot of determination," he said.

He got his first start in the Wood brothers' Dodge in the Rebel 400 at Darlington. He passed Richard Petty to take the lead with twelve laps left. Desperate to get the lead back, Petty lost control, brushed the wall and fell back, giving Pearson the victory.

Critics claimed that the Wood brothers' fine car had won the race, not Pearson. Foyt had already won big events at Daytona and Ontario. It was clear Pearson would have to do more than Foyt had done with this team to set himself apart.

Pearson was ready. He dueled Bobby Isaac in the late stages of the Winston 500 at Talladega, dodged an accident that destroyed Isaac's car and went on to win. He fought off Richard Petty and Bobby Allison for the final 50 miles of the Firecracker 400 at Daytona to win by four feet. He gained and regained the lead six times from Allison in the last 70 miles of the Yankee 400 in Michigan and won by two car-lengths. He also won the Motor State 400 in Michigan and the Delaware 500 at Dover. Pearson entered only 17 races in 1972, but he won six—all on super-speedways. He finished in the first five in twelve races and brought in more than $135,000 in prizes.

In 1973, A.J. Foyt left the Wood brothers' team to

concentrate on racing in the USAC championship cars. Suddenly David Pearson was the top driver on stock car racing's top team. And he had the greatest single season in stock car history.

He broke down in the Daytona 500, the one big race which continued to elude him. But then he started a remarkable winning streak in the Carolina 500. He led 491 out of 492 laps, although he beat Cale Yarborough by a scant four seconds. The Atlanta 500 was easy. He won it by two laps. He led the last 176 laps of a demolition derby in the Rebel 500 at Darlington. An early accident wiped out 20 cars and only 12 of 40 starters finished. Pearson picked his way through the debris and finished first by 13 laps, the widest margin in super-speedway history.

Week after week, he won each NASCAR event in its turn until he had nine in a row. Then in the World 600 at Charlotte his streak ended when he lost to Buddy Baker by two seconds. He bounced back to win the Mason-Dixon 500 in Delaware. Then after passing up events in Texas and California, he returned to win the Motor State 400 in Michigan, the Firecracker 400 in Florida and the Dixie 500 in Atlanta.

All in all, David won eleven races, ten of them on the super-speedways, forever silencing the critics who claimed he couldn't win on the big tracks. He won $215,000 and increased his career earnings to more than one million dollars. He was the second stock car racer and only the sixth in any kind of racing to break the million-dollar barrier. His run of nine victories on nine different tracks in ten starts is regarded as the greatest ever in stock car racing.

His dark, curly hair streaked with gray, Li'l David had

become the dominant driver on the circuit. He did not seem to be changed by his success any more than he had been changed by years of frustration. He went home to his wife and three sons in Spartanburg every chance he had. He lived there quietly except when he was roaring over the backroads with his buddies on one of his several motorcycles.

It was said he owned half his hometown. He shrugged and said, "I don't drink, so I don't go to parties. I don't throw away my money, I invest it, because if something happens to me I don't want my family to lack for anything."

His eldest son had gotten hooked on racing, too, and became the second Pearson to pursue gold and glory in a race car. "I guess I'm getting old when I find myself racing my own son," Li'l David smiled. "But I'm not so old I want to quit and sit in a rockin' chair yet. The money doesn't mean much to me. I've had more than I can spend for a long time now. The glory doesn't mean much to me. I can live without the press clippings and big talk. I have my pride. I know I've proven myself. Mainly, I jus' love a race, especially one I win."

At the end of the 1973 season, David Pearson was second in the all-time standings with 77 Grand National victories and a million dollars in purses. He was first in super-speedway wins with 23. But he was perhaps only just beginning.

When the 1974 season opened, Pearson was approaching his fortieth birthday, but age didn't seem to slow him down. In the Rebel 500 at Darlington, he ran out of gas on the last lap, but had enough of a lead to coast home in front. Then, in a series of sizzling duels with Richard

A jaunty winner in Victory Lane after the 1973 Firecracker 400, David Pearson has grown from a giant-killer to a giant.

Petty, Li'l David won the World 600, the Firecracker 400 and the National 500. Before the season was over, he had won seven super-speedway classics, giving him a total of 30 in his career.

Perhaps his victory over Richard Petty in the 1974 Firecracker 400, one of the most dramatic in the history of the sport, best sums up David Pearson's great courage and ability. David led going into the last lap, but Petty tagged his Dodge to the rear bumper of David's Mercury and was ready to sling-shot past him in the stretch.

In the 1974 Firecracker, Pearson crosses the finish line a few feet ahead of Richard Petty after double-crossing him on the last lap.

Knowing that Petty would not attempt to pass him until the fourth turn, Pearson slowed suddenly entering the first turn—so suddenly that Petty had to swerve inside to avoid hitting him. Pearson let Petty roar past, then fell in behind him. On the fourth turn it was Pearson who pulled out and shot into the lead like a stone in the biblical David's sling-shot.

Glen Wood said, "It was the slickest trick I ever saw in racing."

Richard Petty wasn't as admiring. "It was a danged dangerous thing to do," he said, "and it's not like David to do something like that."

The terrific tactical race between stock car racing's two greatest stars had nearly 100,000 fans standing and cheering in Daytona, where the big cars first became big in sports. "Hey, I'll tell you somethin'," the winner said as he stepped wearily from his steaming machine. "There's nothin' in the world to top this."

INDEX

Page numbers in italics refer to photographs.

149